A LITTLE PIECE OF CUBA

Praise for A Little Piece of Cuba

"The perfect read for anyone who loves rich origin stories, Cuban history, and the warm glow of hearing it all over cafe con leche and maduros at abuelita's kitchen table."

—Brooke Siem, author of *May Cause Side Effects*

"A memoir rich with cultural and political narratives and threaded with an intense yearning to belong."

—Madhushree Ghosh, author of *Khabaar: An Immigrant Journey of Food, Memory and Family*

"Barbara Caver beautifully recounts her journey to reclaim her Cuban-American identity. Her lyrical prose creates a rich narrative encompassing family tradition, cuisine, culture, and history. The result is a story as warm, lively, and colorful as the streets of modern-day Havana, where family memories beckon at every turn. It is a memoir that will resonate with anyone who has struggled to understand their family's past and embrace their place in it."

—Vicki Mayk, author of *Growing Up On The Gridiron: Football, Friendship, and the Tragic Life of Owen Thomas*

"A heartfelt memoir of identity, memory, and rediscovery, *A Little Piece of Cuba* captures one woman's journey from South Carolina to Havana—and from uncertainty to belonging—as she reclaims her Cuban heritage through language, food, family stories, and five unforgettable days in the land her ancestors once called home."

—Alicia M. Rodriguez, author of T*he Shaman's Wife: A Mystical Journey of Surrender and Self-Discovery*

A LITTLE PIECE OF CUBA

A Journey to Become Cubana-Americana

Barbara Caver

SHE WRITES PRESS

Published in 2025 by

She Writes Press, an imprint of The Stable Book Group

32 Court Street, Suite 2109
Brooklyn, NY 11201
https://shewritespress.com

Library of Congress Control Number: 2025912938
ISBN: 979-8-89636-014-8
eISBN: 979-8-89636-015-5

Interior designer: Katherine Lloyd, The DESK

Printed in the United States

Names and identifying characteristics have been changed to protect the privacy of certain individuals.

For my grandmother Carmelina del Valle

Un beso from Baby Barbara

This book is a memoir. The events are portrayed to the best of the author's memory. This work reflects the author's present recollections of experiences over time. Some names, characteristics, and identifying details have been changed to protect the privacy of the people involved. Some dialogue has been recreated.

Contents

Five Days in Havana

Nothing interesting ever happens in an airport. Except in Cuba.

I boarded a plane in New York City in 2017 and three hours later, I walked into an airport hangar in Havana in 1961. Maybe this is what all the travel guides and blogs meant when they said that Cuba was frozen in time. Having made the reverse jump to hyperspace with me, my husband Todd adjusted his sunglasses and followed me down the steps. His wrinkled forehead declared how hard he was trying to suck up the sudden onslaught from the Caribbean heat. This baking linoleum limbo with its lines of tourists at customs and the currency exchange was the last threshold to cross on our way to five days of adventure in a forbidden land. Ready to see for myself if the myth of Havana matched the reality, but also needing to find patience and maybe a little shade, I closed my eyes and inhaled. A sudden swirl of familiar rolled over me.

Sunbaked dirt and concrete.

Coffee and caramelizing sugar.

Zinc oxide and a towel, damp after a swim in the ocean.

The smells sent me time traveling again: this time, into my own memories of the bubbling fountain in my grandmother's walled garden, of my grandfather's rapid-fire Spanish, of the taste of savory black beans. I had been standing in Cuba for about seven minutes and was experiencing something like my life flashing before my eyes. What the hell was going on?

"Todd, this place smells familiar," I said.

"The airport?" he answered.

Sixty-five years before I set foot in José Martí Airport, my mother Carmen was born in Havana, the first child and oldest daughter of Carlos and Carmelina del Valle. In May 1959, she was seven years old when her parents took her and her four younger siblings on vacation in the United States. They never returned to Cuba. In September 1979, twenty years after my mom left, I was born in Augusta, Georgia, just over the state line with South Carolina, the place where my father was born, the place where my parents settled after their marriage, and the place I consider my first home.

When I stepped off that plane onto José Martí Airport's tarmac, I was thirty-seven, the first of my grandparents' direct descendants to visit, and probably the whitest Cuban you ever met. At that moment I had to admit that for most of my life, I had no clue what it meant to be Cuban. My knowledge of Cuba felt like a parlor trick at best—"watch the girl from South Carolina order *café con leche*!"—or an uncomfortable stereotype at worst—"check the box for Hispanic on your college application and get some scholarship money," knowing that the jig would be up as soon as anyone asked me to count beyond twenty. I could give you a list of my favorite foods and a few cute Spanglish words. I know the basic rules of dominoes, I know not to call Grandma when the Dodgers are playing, and I can tell you who Alicia Alonso is (she put Cuban ballet on the map!). I know beyond the shadow of a doubt that Vicks VapoRub cures everything from sore throats to muscle strains to dry cuticles to liver failure to bad days at work. I am dysfunctional without strong coffee first thing in the morning. I abhor cigars, I prefer whisky to rum, and I sunburn under a full moon.

Growing up in South Carolina, having Cuban heritage meant that I was different, and I understood without being told that it was important *not* to be different. Drinking coffee and eating black beans were fine, speaking Spanish maybe not. This weighed heavy on me, already feeling behind the curve as a female child, but how could I deny something that was clearly a part of me? If all I knew about Cuban culture was ballerinas and coffee, maybe that was a good way to be different but not too different. I was pretty young when I found myself on a merry-go-round of unanswered questions: why is it so bad to be different? Isn't there more to Cuba than coffee, Castro, communism, and rum? Cuba was like a puzzle I was trying to put together. Pieces connected painstakingly over time, but I never *ever* thought to call myself "Cuban" or "Cuban American." I rarely said, "I have Cuban heritage."

When I was seventeen, I moved from South Carolina to New York City for college, and in a similar fashion to what my mother experienced, I never went back. Those early years in New York were an odyssey for me as I transitioned away from a parochial Southern home and settled into a big city life all on my own. I found myself hypnotized by the city's vibrant cultural diversity and drooling over the gastronomic wonderland that New York offers. Hiding my Southern penchant for florals and hot pink behind a monochromatic city girl wardrobe, I walked, bussed, and rode the subway all over the five boroughs—yes, all five!—sometimes accompanied by a gaggle of fellow NYU students or visiting friends in search of interesting sites and new food to try.

"She's eating up the world," my non-Cuban, Southern-born father, Tony, said about my culinary tourism. Food was my favorite way of exploring new cultures and meeting new people, and Cuban food was high on the list of things to try since my mother never made it at home. My grandmother did, so I knew enough to be dangerous and wasn't shy when it came to ordering in Cuban restaurants. I also really enjoyed passing swift and effective judgment on whether the food was good or not, thinking that maybe I had Cuban genes after all, they were just concentrated in my stomach.

Perhaps because I had overwhelmed my system with so much *arroz con pollo* (a savory stew made with a whole chicken, rice, and saffron) that it was practically venting out of my pores, I suddenly started meeting Cubans all over my New York life, from classmates in college to colleagues at my first job to people at the gym and neighbors down the street. Before I knew anything at all about the Cuban connection, I picked up on an easygoing manner and felt a comfortable rapport. Maybe we had a similar class schedule and they had told me their mother was named Barbara too. Maybe, after weeks of noticing that we frequented the same coffee spot at the same time of day, we struck up a conversation in the elevator at the office. Maybe my morning commute got me to the gym a few minutes early one day and I had time to chat with some of the people I'd been sweating next to for months. Sometimes they had been in my orbit for a while, sometimes we had just been introduced, but they always seemed like a person I'd like to know better. Then, over the course of a few months or a few minutes, Cuba would work its way in, maybe because they had remarked that I didn't seem to have much of a Southern accent, or maybe they volunteered their Cuban connection as a way to explain why this coffee spot was their favorite. It didn't matter how long or how the connection revealed itself; once we knew that Cuba was bringing us together, the casual conversation was scuttled and we were two long lost friends reuniting. Grins spread across faces, hands reached out to take my hand or pat a shoulder, heads tilted or eyes squinted as if to bring the Cuban in me into focus. The biggest, and most bewildering, response I ever got was a full-on bear hug and a jubilant shout, "Oh you're Cuban? That explains a lot!" Good, I guess?

The reaction was always a mix of welcoming joy and curiosity, and also my cue to shut up and listen as they explained to me how they were connected to Cuba. These were people whose lives and identities were shaped by Cuba in ways that mine was not; some had family there and visited frequently, some switched effortlessly from English to Spanish, some had grown up in Cuban exile communities around the world. And nothing about Cuba was off limits; we talked about everything from the Mariel Boatlift to *platanos* (the giant green bananas that are a staple of Caribbean cuisine). They gave me pieces of my Cuba puzzle to fit into place, and everything mattered, from simple things like how to perfect homemade *maduros* (*platanos* cooked in a specific way to carmelize them) to deeper, more culturally specific things like the connection between Saint Barbara, familiar to me from my Catholic upbringing, and Changó, the *orisha* or god of thunder in Santería. Every December 4, Cuba honors both Saint Barbara and Changó together, something I don't think I would have learned without moving to New York and meeting other Cubans. No one ever flinched or corrected me when I fumbled over Spanish or pronounced words incorrectly in my Southern-laced Spanglish. In fact, they encouraged me to use what I did know and try to do more to connect to my Cuban heritage. To them, I was Cuban. End of story. Though they all came from different backgrounds and different parts of Cuba and the United States, their messages that welcomed and challenged me were so similar that it was hard not to think that there was a higher power sending them as guides to lead me back to Cuba, like the ghosts in *A Christmas Carol* are sent to guide Ebenezer Scrooge towards redemption. I came to think of this angelic force as a character called Sara the Real Cuban, a shapeshifter who would appear to me in many forms—male, female, old, young, teacher, friend, neighbor—to show me incredible compassion and understanding at a time when I felt lost and confused about my heritage. Despite the many forms she took, Sara the Real Cuban always embodied the spirit of Cuba, a child of exiles carrying her culture in her bones, using it to fuel the strength with which she takes on the world, and generously guiding me toward a different, deeper understanding of myself as a Cuban American.

Throughout my early life, Cuba hid in plain sight, from *arroz con frijoles* (black beans and rice) served at my grandparents' house to my own name, Carmelina Barbara Caver. The Cuban things were always served with a sidecar of a not-Cuban thing, which taught me how not to hide it but not be too obvious about it. My generation of grandchildren called my grandfather *Abuelito,* but we called my grandmother *Grandma,* not *Abuela.* And because she lived in Louisiana and my brother and I lived in South Carolina, the two of us called her "Grandma Faraway." In my immediate family, we called our hot coffee with hot milk *café au lait* not *café con leche*, although it was made in the microwave with Maxwell House instant coffee, so I'm not sure it qualified as *café* anything. Living in New York, a city that boldly celebrates diversity, with Sara the Real Cuban popping up all over the place, I felt encouraged to reflect on these Cuban-themed pieces of my identity. Something Cuban was there; maybe I had to chip away at the patina to find it, like an archaeologist carefully dusting off ancient shards. Slowly my Cuba puzzle was coming together, but what would complete it? I had a list of hoops I thought I needed to jump through:

Learn to speak Spanish? (maybe)

Learn to cook more Cuban dishes? (never a bad idea)

Use more Vicks? (always)

Drink more rum? (blech, definitely not)

And then Sara the Real Cuban asked me, “Have you ever been to Cuba?”

What?! No! was my kneejerk reaction, but my curiosity trounced my shock and I said back to her, “No . . . have you?”

I thought I would go to the moon before I went to Cuba. I couldn’t picture it as a real place. No one in my family expressed a desire to go. Not at all. Once, my mother said something like, “Cuba is communist now.” Say no more, Mom. I was born in September 1979 when the word *communist* still meant danger in American society. Learning about the travel restrictions for Americans due to the long-standing embargo only underscored the idea that Cuba was enemy territory. Approach at your own peril.

But going to Cuba was different for Sara. She took trips to see her aunts and uncles in a suburb of Havana as easily and casually as I took trips to see my aunts and uncles in Louisiana. She didn’t have to travel through Canada or Mexico like many Americans did. Her passport was stamped with Cuban visas that she presented to US Customs and Border Patrol upon return. This did not sound at all like sneaking behind enemy lines. But I explained it away: *Sara the Real Cuban has family in Havana*, which meant that Cuba was accessible to her in a way that it wasn’t to me. But once challenged, I couldn’t shake the question of going to Cuba and seeing it for myself. It took a while for me to take action; though I was bursting with curiosity about Cuba, I kept the idea of a visit at arm’s length. It seemed safer to hide behind the red tape of travel restrictions than to face my inner tug-of-war: “Am I Cuban, or am I not?” If I set foot on Cuban ground, I would have to answer that question.

I hemmed and hawed. I sidestepped questions about my Cuban heritage. Then the Obama administration rolled back travel restrictions for Americans going to Cuba, and suddenly, it was *the* place to go. Everyone I knew was hopping on cruise ships and planes bound for Havana. They spent a few days riding around in 1950s vintage cars, drinking mojitos, and getting sunburned. They returned with cigars slipped through customs and a bottle of *authentic* Havana Club. I listened to friends of friends and colleagues and casual acquaintances describe how their cruise ship docked for a few hours in Havana before moving on to another sun-drenched, rum-soaked Caribbean playground. There they went, casually checking off exotic locations on their bucket list without ever really taking the place in.

These stories pissed me off. I wanted to shake these people hard and scream that Cuba wasn't a sideshow to be splashed across Facebook. I didn't want to admit to myself that these selfie stick–wielding idiots knew more about Cuba than I did because they let a cruise ship take them there. They downed the government propaganda like a Bacardi shot and did not experience anything of what Cuba really was. *It was not fair.* This was my family's homeland from which they exiled themselves, but I didn't feel any more Cuban than these tourists in their sunglasses and sturdy shoes. So, what the hell, why not join the casual ranks of tourists and hop on that three-hour JetBlue flight from JFK to Havana to get another stamp on my passport? The worst-case scenario was I'd come home and everything would be the same: I would still not speak Spanish, I would still feel squeamish calling myself Cuban American, and I would still use Vicks VapoRub to cure everything. I had convinced myself that I was so un-Cuban that the best thing a visit to Cuba would give me was the right to say that I had been.

But as soon as Todd and I arrived, I felt Cuba inviting me in, just as I always felt invited into my Cuban grandparents' house when we visited. Grandma Faraway's house was unlike any house I'd ever seen, and I was always fascinated by how I entered it. One story high, the house was shaped like an *L* around Grandma's garden courtyard with its fountain centerpiece. A formal, yet seldom used, entrance faced the street, and a high brick wall closed off the garden on two sides, turning the *L*-shape into a box and hiding the garden from the outside world. A wrought iron gate next to the garage allowed passage through the brick wall from the driveway into the garden. To a girl with a vibrant imagination, this was a better secret garden than the one in the book. Pulling myself out of the car after a two-day drive, I heard the bubbling fountain and immediately felt calmer. I would scurry to the wrought iron gate and that's when Grandma appeared. On one visit, I remember her in a bright floral dress that flared to her knees and casual yet classy espadrilles. She looked like a magical garden fairy, skipping toward us with youthful athleticism, moving aside the gate, kneeling, and throwing her arms open to me and my brother.

"Barbara!" she exclaimed, pronouncing my name as she always did with three syllables. *Bar-bar-a*. "John!" and we were absorbed into a big welcoming hug.

That was exactly how Cuba welcomed me, skipping toward me with arms wide open, opening the gates, and letting me in to a secret place. Cuba did not see me as a rank-and-file tourist with a selfie stick and sensible shoes. Cuba recognized me and accepted me as one of her own. This foreign place, this enemy territory, this embargoed land was just . . . home.

A few hours later, a taxi dropped Todd and me on Calle 17 near Parque John Lennon. This Airbnb was our home for the next five days. Punishing heat tried to melt us, and in five minutes, I surrendered a full layer of epidermis to the sun. Next door, a black-market beer distributor was in high gear. I spotted a case of Blue Moon and immediately salivated at the thought of icy cold beer.

A young woman in a sundress greeted us. Swap espadrilles for the pink flip flops and she would have been Grandma Faraway from years ago.

"Hi, my name is Madeleine. Maddy. How was your flight?"

Oh! I thought, surprised. *I understand her Spanish.*

"Hi . . . it's nice to meet you . . . the trip . . . good, thanks," I fumbled through the sentence, thinking carefully about each word and practically vibrating with self-consciousness. But I got my point across. Her sweet smile widened and I sighed in relief.

Maddy's house was located in Havana's Vedado neighborhood, a central district known for its impressive culinary scene, vibrant nightlife, and beautiful mansions in various stages of either destruction or restoration, depending on your point of view. Vedado means *forbidden*, a really good word to describe Cuba, I thought. After Cuba's liberation from Spain in the 1890s, the country's modern society centered itself in Vedado, and by the time Fidel Castro came through, Vedado had blossomed into the cosmopolitan capital of Cuba and an international destination. My family had property in Vedado before the revolution, so I decided to situate us there. Slightly outside of the tourist area, Vedado might give us a snapshot of current Havana life. I also didn't admit it to myself but I was hoping to feel a real connection to my Cuban ancestors by basing ourselves in an area that they literally used to own. I didn't expect to feel that connection so soon, but as Maddy led us up to the Airbnb on the roof, I saw the tiles and the "forbidden" became familiar.

Beautifully crafted tiles painted with flowers and triangles in bright reds, striking blues, rich browns, and vibrant greens decorated the concrete steps leading up to the roof. In the apartment, tiles were everywhere, arranged in charming mosaics on the floor, the kitchen counter, the bathroom. Suddenly, I was nine years old standing in the doorway of my grandparents' kitchen in their house in Louisiana, twenty-nine years after they left Cuba, watching Grandma Faraway move around. I was barefoot, and she had on a dark blue apron over another sundress. I traced with my big toe the thick white boundary between the tiles on the floor. The ball of my foot tapped on the colorful interlocking triangles, and Grandma smiled at me. No matter how hot it was in Louisiana, those tiles were always cool, and as I ran my hand over the backsplash in Havana, I felt the same coolness.

Maddy showed me how the keys worked and confirmed the time for our breakfast the next day. With the logistics sorted, I pointed at the tiles. "*Qué linda,*" I said. How pretty.

I didn't think her smile could grow any wider, but it did. "Thank you. I'm downstairs if you need anything. Enjoy your stay."

She left, and I turned to Todd, half expecting him to have stuck his head in the fridge, but he stood like a statue in the middle of the apartment and stared at me.

"You're going to think I'm nuts," I said, "but these tiles look exactly like the tiles in my grandmother's kitchen."

"You understood everything she said," he said. "And you answered in Spanish!"

I laughed. I wouldn't call that speaking Spanish. Yes, I understood the broad strokes of what Maddy was saying, and I was able to respond after carefully thinking through what to say. I know I made lots of mistakes and butchered the language like a pig, but Maddy never once grew frustrated or corrected me.

When I said *"qué linda"* about the tiles, I was repeating a phrase that my grandmother used a lot. I first heard her say it when I was around ten years old. I was dressed in my flower girl dress for my godfather's wedding and Grandma said, "*Qué linda,* Barbara, how pretty." She often followed up Spanish with English when her non-Spanish-speaking grandchildren were around, so I picked up a bit by observation and careful listening. Here I was in Cuba, using Spanish to the best of my ability, and Cuba herself was gently winking at me, urging me along. Fumbling my way through, parroting phrases that I'd heard before, using the feminine form for *spouse* when referring to Todd, and constructing the phrases in my head before speaking . . . it was all fine because I was trying. I wasn't going to magically or spontaneously burst into Spanish, but Maddy's cadence and the practical nature of our conversation carried a lilt of familiarity that gave me just a little boost of confidence, even if I sounded like a toddler.

As we unpacked and settled in, I noticed more and more things that reminded me of Grandma Faraway's house. The ceramic soap dish in the bathroom, the patio furniture on the terrace, the way the windows squeaked as they cranked open . . . I was flooded with a sense of the familiar and a growing connection between me and this so-called forbidden place. It was becoming clear that Cuba and I had a very strong connection, and Cuba was not-so-gently nudging me to explore it.

After Todd and I slathered on SPF 55, we walked up Avenida 23, better known by its prerevolutionary name La Rampa, to the Hotel Nacional de Cuba and the Malecón. Meandering along the famous sea wall in the late afternoon, we lost ourselves in the spirit and vibe of Havana. With the colonial era Spanish fort Castillo de los Tres Reyes del Morro in the background, a lone trumpeter played the theme from *The Godfather*, a nod to Havana's past as a mafia den. We bought two homemade ice cream cones from a street vendor as a snack. As the sun was setting, a tiny wiener dog appeared. We thought the dog would beg for food, but he (it was very obvious that the dog was a he) appeared to be waiting for us to follow him. Our dog-guide walked ahead of us towards Vedado and left us in front of a small restaurant, one that wasn't starred in red sharpie on my Streetwise map. Because tourists should always take the recommendations of the locals, especially the four-legged ones, we stepped into the restaurant. I answered "*Sí, gracias*" when the host greeted us with a gracious smile and offered to sit us at a low table by a high-arched window framing the Malecón and the Caribbean Sea.

I don't speak Spanish until it's time to order food, and then I become quite the linguist. *"Dos mojitos y croquetas de jamon, por favor,* and . . . this one." I pointed out *pescado*-something on the menu and a few minutes later, two mojitos, ham and cheese fritters, and a platter of grilled shellfish appeared. Colorful cars zipped along the Malecón, their big fins flashing like sunlight on the ocean waves. I snapped a few photos with one hand while sipping a mojito with the other, not even bothering to stand up from my comfortable seat. The sun was setting as I tipped the bowl of *tres leches* cake on its side to get every last drop of *leche* onto my spoon. A large moon watched over us as we strolled back to Maddy's house.

The following morning promptly at nine o'clock, in a direct contradiction to the tardiness known as Cuban time, we heard a cheery, "*Buenos días!*" from downstairs. Maddy and her husband appeared on the shady roof to deliver a large breakfast tray with hot *café con leche*, scrambled eggs, ham, fresh Cuban bread, butter, and papaya. Sufficiently fueled, we descended the tiled stairs and crossed the street to Parque John Lennon. A lifelike statue of John Lennon seated on a bench is the park's centerpiece, and Todd, a diehard Beatles fan, couldn't resist a few selfies with the music icon's likeness. From Calle 17, we turned left on Avenida Paseo.

That's when Todd asked me, "Aren't the family homes supposed to be around here?"

I had a photo of a palatial white mansion built by my great-great-grandfather Pablo Mendoza. My great-grandmother María Mendoza lived here, and my mother Carmen referred to this palace simply as "my grandmother's house." All I knew was that the house was in Vedado; I didn't have an address.

"I don't know how we are going to find it," I fussed to Todd as we stopped at a street corner to wait out the traffic light. Todd and I are New Yorkers with strong jaywalking skills, but outside of the five boroughs, we wait for the light to cross the street.

I was suddenly *not* interested in genealogical spelunking, not when there was a lot more food, music, sights, and experiences to take in. The Malecón was straight ahead and we only had five days. It's not as if finding a house was going to tell me anything about my heritage that I didn't already know. I am pretty sure I muttered, "House, what house?" then launched into a full-voiced rant as I looked down the street to my right for traffic, "I don't want to spend our time wandering around looking for a house. I want to take in all we can of Havana while we're here. Maybe I'll come back one day and can do the family archeological dig but for now, I—hey!"

I had turned my head left to look for traffic and my rant died in my throat. A memory had come to life right in front of me.

"There it is! There's the house! That's the courtyard!" my voice escalated with each sentence until I was shouting. This wasn't far off from what I used to say when Grandma Faraway's house would come into view.

In my childhood home in South Carolina, there was a formal living room in the front of the house that we barely used. Above the nice oak bookshelves with a complete set of *Encyclopedia Britannica* and the record player with *Willie Nelson's Greatest Hits* on repeat, next to the elegant JCPenney sofa too stiff to be comfortable, my mother had hung a small copy of a painting from Cuba. When visitors asked about the painting, I knew enough to answer, "That's Cuba, where my mom is from." The image showed an alabaster statue of a shy yet naked lady in a well-tended tropical garden. The artist had painted a white angelic glow around the statue, but that didn't stop my brother John and me from sneaking into the living room to enjoy an occasional laugh at the lady's expense: "What are you doing running around the backyard nekkid as a jaybird?"

Now I saw the painting in real life, replicated exactly how I remembered it down to the angelic halo. I grabbed the bars of the tall wrought iron fence separating me from my memory and stared. Then I noticed the tiles that ran along the curved stone base where the fence met the sidewalk. I followed the tiles like Dorothy followed the yellow brick road and I came face-to-face with a tall gate crowned by a giant styled *M. M* for Mendoza, my great-grandmother's maiden name.

A security guard emerged from a station inside the gate. Alternating between baby Spanish and useless English, I did my best to explain that I was visiting from the United States (I'm pretty sure I said *Etats-Unis*, the French name, not *Estados Unidos*) and that this was my great-great-grandfather's house (I said *abuelo* four times in quick succession with a bunch of charade-like hand gestures to demonstrate the passage of time), and I asked to take a few photos. I'm sure the guard didn't understand, let alone believe, a word of what I said, but he was very friendly and showed us where to position our cameras between the bars of the gate for better views of the house itself. I caught every third word but managed to connect the dots as he described the house's special features and explained that it was now the residence of the British ambassador to Cuba. Occasionally, the royal family visited, something social media confirmed with a photo of Charles and Camilla in a convertible on the circular drive. That photo was taken just a few weeks before our visit.

Language barriers be damned, Todd asked the guard for recommendations of local restaurants and music venues. This was Todd's signature move, often resulting in our best experiences and fondest memories while traveling. While the guard pointed and pantomimed at Todd's map, I stared dumbfounded at the house. I realized I was looking not at the building itself but for something invisible, for a personal connection to this palatial house with its gleaming marble statues and fancy courtyard. Had my grandfather come here as a toddler to swim in the pool and chase lizards around the garden? Were there photos of my grandfather's parents at this house, maybe for an engagement party or Easter brunch? Which room was my great-grandmother's childhood bedroom, and did she have a lot of toys? Did she have thick hair like mine that couldn't decide if it was curly or just plain bushy? Was she short, like me and most of the women in my family, or did she get the recessive tall lady genes? I may have occasionally thought about ancestors in Cuba, but I'd never before thought about them as real people who had favorite foods and quirks and crankiness. Yet here was the solid, mansion-sized proof of a lineage that was layered and deep.

Thanking the guard, we returned to Avenida Paseo and shared our amazement at the serendipity of finding the Mendoza House a few blocks from where I'd randomly booked our Airbnb. Later that afternoon after a long walk along the Malecón to Habana Vieja, we found a bar owned by English expats and settled into the air conditioning to compare our photos over *bocados y cerveza*. Todd showed me his glamorous photo of the Mendoza House; the angle was slightly low, and the white facade glowed in the mid-morning sun.

"That's a great shot," I said.

"Check your camera," he said. "You were right next to me, and your camera is better."

I flipped through my camera and gasped. Taken side by side at the same time, my photo was identical to Todd's except for one eerie feature: there was a ghostly orb in mine. Enlarging the photo, I thought the orb looked strangely like a face. It hovered near the front door, as if someone came out to greet us.

"Is there a family resemblance?" Todd joked.

"I think it's my great-great-grandmother, and yes, she

recognized me." I don't believe in ghosts, but I was damn near certain about this. "People say I look like my mom, right?"

Todd didn't even have to agree with that. When my mom and I stand side by side, even though she's tan with dark hair, strangers easily identify us as mother and daughter.

"So, my mom looks like her father," I continued, "and this house was owned by his mother's father, so . . ." I propped my sunglasses at the end of my nose and chirped in an affected voice, "*¡Mira, Pablo! ¡Aquí!* You'll never believe this! There is an American woman outside the gate right now! She is one of ours, I know it! *¡Ay, Dios!*"

Todd and I shared a laugh and ordered more food and bottled water.

It was the first time I had ever thought of myself as having a Cuban face, but I didn't linger on that thought. I recalled seeing a photo or two of my great-grandmother María Mendoza del Valle in an album, but I couldn't pull the image of her face into my mind. Is there a family resemblance, and who carries it now? Does my mom look like her, do I, or does one of my cousins? All I know of María Mendoza del Valle is that she was my grandfather's mother and she moved to Mexico City after leaving Cuba. My mother Carmen and her sisters visited María as teenagers during the summers, and I once found myself in tears from laughing at my aunt Elena recounting the hijinks three teenage girls got up to when they visited their grandmother in Mexico. Did my Abuelito, the strong patriarch I knew and feared until his death in 2006, drive his mother crazy with his antics as a child? Did she need a strong cup of coffee first thing in the morning just like me? Did she ever see Alicia Alonso's performance of *Giselle*? When was Vicks VapoRub invented, and how much did she have in her medicine cabinet? Standing in front of the Mendoza House, I didn't see a historic example of pre-Castro Cuba or a vanished aristocracy long past its prime.

I saw traces of the people who lived and moved in this space. I saw my family and my ancestors. How do I fit in here? And how do I fit in with this place now?

On the flight back home to New York, I wrote in my diary, "Now that I've been to Cuba . . . am I Cuban or not?" I then scratched out the "or not." It was an important first step on a personal journey to examine my past experiences, bring my heritage into my present, and start to rewrite it for my future. After five days in Havana, there was no going back to "not Cuban." I may not be what I think a Cuban should be, but if people are composed of a lot of different things, then I am a mosaic, like the sturdy tiles on the floor of my grandmother's kitchen and on Maddy's staircase. And there is a part of me that has always been Cuban. It was time to make sure that part was dusted off, polished up, and placed on a windowsill in the sun.

¿Habla Español?

Cuban Americans are defined as individuals born in Cuba who immigrated to the United States.

My mom.

Cuban Americans are also defined as individuals born in the United States who trace one parent's origins to Cuba.

Me.

So, I am Cuban American, even though I don't speak Spanish.

"That's not unusual for the children of immigrants and exiles in the United States. And for the second generation of a country like Cuba, not speaking the language at all is the norm, not an exception," Sara the Real Cuban once told me. "You're not alone."

But that didn't help. A week or so before my trip to Cuba, I woke up around two in the morning in a cold sweat. I had been dreaming of Cuba, photoshopping myself against a collage of what I imagined it would be like. It took a while to realize that something was wrong: I had no voice. Totally mute. No vocal chords. In Cuba, I apparently thought I couldn't speak at all.

Unlike the generation of Cubans that my mom would have been a part of if she had grown up there, most Cubans now don't speak English, and we were purposefully avoiding tourist hotels and arranged tours where English might be more prevalent. We were entering an English desert, where Todd and I would be on our own with my infantile Spanish as our only form of communication. I imagined Sara the Real Cuban letting out a sigh and maybe saying to me, "Language barriers never stopped you from traveling before, and not being able to speak Thai didn't induce a panic attack four days before your honeymoon!"

She was right, of course; in fact, I usually thought the language was part of the adventure in a foreign place. No, the tossing and turning over speaking Spanish in Cuba had nothing to do with travel to a new place; it had to do with old wounds.

Ask me why I don't speak Spanish and I see ghosts: vaguely half-answered questions about my family's move to the United States and why I was raised with a cavernous disconnection from my mother's homeland. Limited exposure to Spanish came through family visits, but I was never immersed or instructed. My grandmother spoke to my father and me in English but to my mother in Spanish, sometimes in the same sentence. The only times I ever heard my mother speak Spanish were when she was speaking to her parents and siblings in person, never on the phone, and even then, sometimes she answered in English and the whole conversation shifted away from Spanish. Hearing and seeing my mother speak Spanish was like magic to me, so I wanted to learn.

I picked up a few charming vocabulary words which I pronounced boldly yet terribly, such as *desayuno* (breakfast), *cosita* (trinket), *paleta* (popsicle or ice cream cone), and—one of my favorites—*vámanos* (let's go!). I once asked my grandfather to teach me a full sentence in Spanish. What he taught me was a very useful complete sentence: *El gato es muy gordo.* The cat is very fat. Once when my grandmother was serving black beans and rice, my aunt Barbara told me that if I wanted to speak Spanish, I should count the black beans in Spanish as I ate them. I did count the beans as high as I could go, which was the number twenty. After two helpings of black beans and rice, I still could only count to twenty.

I felt like I was being humored, not educated, but it didn't stop me from trying.

"Hey mom," I might say on a car ride home from school, "how do you say *horse* in Spanish?"

"*Caballo*," came the response from the driver's seat. My mom drove our 1989 Chevrolet with one hand on the wheel and the other hand twirling a lock of her thick dark hair. She had learned to drive a stick shift so when automatic transmission became the norm, she still drove the car with one hand.

"What about *dog?*"

"*Perro*. Do y'all want frozen yogurt?"

She steered one-handed into the drive-through lane of TCBY while John and I repeated "*perro*" over and over again. That was the time we discovered that I can roll my *r*'s and John can't.

But things shifted around the idea of me speaking Spanish as I grew up. My questions were always answered but never elaborated on, and I couldn't shake the feeling that I had pried or asked too much. Getting a few vocabulary words here and there was fine, but when I asked direct questions about speaking Spanish, my mother answered, "You can study Spanish in school" in a tone that told me the matter was closed. For a large talkative family, we didn't want to talk in or about Spanish, so I stuck to the easier questions and left the hard-hitting ones to be answered by my own reasoning and observation.

On another car ride home from tennis practice, my mother taught me and John the phrase *comida de gusanos*. It translates as "worm food." We had been discussing a rival junior tennis team and I had asked for a clever way to trash-talk them without them catching on to what we were saying. A few years later, I was in college when I learned that in Cuba, the word *gusanos* has another meaning. In a famous speech, Fidel Castro referred to people who opposed him as *gusanos*. Worms. It became synonymous with the Cuban wealthy upper classes that Castro ousted, people like my family. I cringed remembering that day in the car on the way to the tennis tournament when John and I got a good laugh repeating the phrase *comida de gusanos* over and over.

As I grew up and my life started to take shape, it was harder and harder to imagine where Cuba and the Spanish language might fit. I was surrounded by things that didn't look Cuban, like our one-story house with its two-car garage and large backyard ruled by the family dog. The house was built for suburban life in South Carolina, whereas Grandma Faraway's *L*-shaped house with its secret garden was very different, even for Louisiana. The inside was different; her formal living room reminded me of a small ballroom, but our living room with the picture of the alabaster nekkid angel was where we kept the furniture that was too fancy to sit on, ignored in favor of the comfortable den with the television that overlooked the dog's domain. Grandma's kitchen floor was made of colorful tiles that stayed cool no matter how hot it was outside. Our kitchen floor was interlocking brown and beige vinyl squares designed to hide sneaker treads, crumbs, and spills. Grandma's house was built to be graceful and exotic, just like Cuba and Spanish, but ours was built for practicality and normalcy.

As a child, I developed this idea that being Cuban and speaking Spanish was *not* normal, and early experiences taught me to proceed with caution when it came to talking about my heritage. Long before I wanted to admit it, I had a Cuban face. I couldn't pretend that I was adopted. When I'm meeting distant relatives for the first time, I'm no longer surprised when they say something like, "Oh, you're definitely Carmen's daughter." Or "I saw you from across the street and I knew you were a del Valle." Or "I'm not sure how we're related but we definitely are." I am a founding member of the famous del Valle Family 5'1" Club, an exclusive all-female group of all ages but only one size.

Despite this unmistakable family resemblance, I also heard, "You don't look Cuban," which confused me. As a young kid, it really hurt too. If I don't look Cuban, but I look like my family and my family is Cuban, then what does that say about me and where I belong? It took me years to find the strength to flip that argument, see the proof in my own face, and ask back, "What is a Cuban supposed to look like?" I bet you most of those people couldn't find Cuba on a map, then or now.

Not speaking Spanish, not looking Cuban . . . each "not" felt like a point deduction on my Cuban card, as if cultural heritage were Olympic gymnastics. What I did have was a Cuban first name: Carmelina, a name I share with my grandmother. Because my grandmother was Cuban, and her name was Carmelina, I thought of the name as distinctly and uniquely Cuban. But at birth it was decided that I would go by my middle name, Barbara, and Carmelina was swept to the side. Just like the stuffy living room closed off to the rest of the house, Carmelina was my seldom-used, unpronounceable, difficult to spell, formal name. It was the name on the passport documents, doctor's offices, school registrars, credit cards, and mortgage statements. Barbara was the name I attached to myself and owned, but I couldn't avoid strangers' curiosity and questions about an unusual name like Carmelina, so for my entire life, mundane and perfunctory tasks like starting fourth grade at a new school, picking up college textbooks, and renewing my driver's license at the DMV have transformed into interrogations about my ancestry and bilingual skills. The conversation is always awkward:

"Carme-LIE-na?" Nice try, Hooked-on-Phonics. It's Carme-LEE-na.

"Carmela?" Nope, that's Tony Soprano's wife. Try again.

"Car-caramel?" It's my name, not an ice cream topping.

"That's a pretty name." Thank you.

"I've never seen a name like that before." How am I supposed to respond to that?

"What kind of name is that?" What kind of name is *yours*, Dan Jones?

"Can I call you something else?" Yes, you can call me Barbara. Does that make you feel better?

When the line at the DMV or the doctor's reception desk is long, that might be the end of it, much to my relief, but occasionally, I am subjected to more torture. While the application is processed or the insurance card copied or the person displays actual curiosity and not just jackass nosiness, I end up explaining to a total stranger—whose name and heritage I know *nothing* about—that my grandmother for whom I am named is from Cuba.

Then the next question might be, "Oh, can you speak Spanish?" I cringe.

Maybe it comes as an assumption: "So you speak Spanish." I can neither confirm nor deny.

Occasionally it's "*¿Habla español?*" and I want to sink through the floor.

No matter how it is asked, my answer is always the same: No. No. No, I don't speak Spanish.

Then, I'm handed my new driver's license, told to take a seat and the doctor will call me, handed my textbooks, thanked for stopping by HR, and the earth continues to rotate. As the bank teller moves on to the next transaction, I ask myself for the nine billionth time: *Why don't I speak Spanish?*

No matter what our kitchen floor looked like or how white my skin was all summer long, the biggest thing that made me feel unsure and insecure about my Cuban heritage was not knowing the answer to that question. *Why don't I speak Spanish?* Without the language, I didn't know how else to legitimize my claim to

Cuba. My insecurity was worsened by a few interactions when I was a kid that were downright hurtful. A classmate's parent once told me it was a "shame" that I never learned how to speak Spanish. With her Puerto Rican husband and bilingual children, she might not have realized that things were different for me with only one parent from Cuba, a country torn by revolution and strife. I don't think she meant to make me feel like this was my fault, but that's exactly how I took it. The concept of shame in that context startled me because I felt like "shame" was a result of me doing something wrong. How was it wrong that I had never learned to speak Spanish? Also, I was nine years old, and as my mother often said, there was time to learn if I wanted to. I immediately cast the shame onto my mother for not working harder to instill the language in me. I silently blamed her for creating all of this trouble for me.

"I never asked to be called Carmelina Barbara, not Barbara Carmelina," I groaned once to Sara the Real Cuban. "My brother's name is John, not Juan. It was like they were designating me as the Cuban flag bearer from birth!"

Moving to New York made it so much easier. For one thing, Carmelina is not a strange name and no one at the DMV even makes eye contact let alone wants to chit chat.

By the time we left for our trip in 2017, I was more comfortable with my names but still not comfortable at all with my Spanish, or lack thereof. But culture is more than just language, and there were customs and rituals that I experienced, unspoken rites just as powerful as language, that were familiar to me. How people interacted with us, how the food tasted, how the whole city quieted down for *siesta* . . . these all brought me comfort and allowed my nerves to settle. *I know these people, this smells like something Grandma made once, it doesn't feel like I'm in a foreign country,* I said to Todd often during our five days in Havana. But because I had to try my best in Spanish, I gained a new appreciation for the challenges of communicating when you can't speak the language, and I realized that no one was a better authority on language immersion than my own mother.

She was barely seven years old when she was thrown into a new world where no one spoke Spanish at a time when English as a Second Language courses didn't exist. The nuns in their first Catholic school in the United States said that if she and her siblings couldn't keep up with elementary school in English, then they would fail and repeat a grade. Maybe because she wanted to prove the nuns wrong, as I would have, or maybe because she understood even as a child that their status as newcomers to a foreign land meant that obstacles were more challenging, my mother did not fail her first year in an American elementary school. The Cuba that my mother was born in fiercely educated its people, so she was smart and, as she told me once about learning English as a child, "I learned fast." But breaking down barriers between my mom and her new community was critical to social survival in the United States, and the first thing that had to go was Spanish. Add to this the dawning realization that her family was not returning to Cuba, and my mom's experience with English as a second language was more like a baptism by fire than a gently immersive study abroad course. The general impression of Cubans arriving in the United States then fell on a spectrum from "refugee" to "exile," and though I stop short of referring to my family as refugees because of their power to choose when and how to leave, I know they experienced rejection and ostracism from the communities where they first settled. And these challenges trickled down to me.

I once heard Abuelito remark that he was surrounded by grandchildren with American accents who don't speak Spanish. Forty years had passed since they left Cuba when he said this, and his matter-of-fact way of stating it said nothing to me about how he really felt about it. Had he realized that one consequence of pushing his children to learn English was that Spanish would be almost erased from the family in less than two generations? I certainly thought my family didn't do nearly enough to pass the language on to me and my generation. Abuelito was the father of six girls and one boy, most of whom married non-Cubans and non-Spanish speakers. But maybe moving away from Cuba, and by extension from Spanish, was the whole point. My mother Carmen del Valle became Carmen Caver, and she moved four states away to her husband's home in South Carolina into a community centered around our church and schools where Spanish was present but not prominent.

Even the way that I say the family name is a comment on how present the language has been in my life. I echoed the pronunciation that my mother used, "del VAH-yay." It is such a common surname that traveling through the south of Spain one summer, my mother and I snapped a photo of a street sign: *Calle del Valle,* which has a singsong rhythm when spoken out loud. There are many ways to say the name, almost as many ways as there are dialects of Spanish. Sometimes the "del" is the main event, sometimes the double-*l* rolls and tumbles, sometimes there is an unfamiliar "zsh" sound thrown in there, but no matter how I heard anyone say it, it was always better and more Spanish than how I said it. Because my way sounded so *not* Spanish, there was a period in my life when I reverted to the 100 percent English version "dell valley," which backfired in a different way when an elementary school classmate singsonged "the farmer in the dell valley" over and over and over again until the daggers shooting out of my eyes finally silenced her.

I had the same experience when I spoke about Abuelito. No one ever corrected me on how to say it, but I could tell that how I said it and how my mother said it were very different, so I started referring to Abuelito by his first name, Carlos. Since Abuela was already Grandma Faraway, I never knew why we called one

Cuban grandparent by a Spanish nickname and the other by an English one. It certainly said a lot about how I viewed each of my grandparents and their relationship to Cuba as I grew up. Abuelito always seemed to be looking back, speaking Spanish to his children, humoring his grandchildren, walking me through the family tree, keeping up with news of Cuba, telling us stories from his life in Cuba, while Grandma Faraway embraced their life in the United States, running the household like the boss of seven children and fourteen grandchildren, involving herself in their local community in Louisiana, fiercely attending the local church, and keeping up with her own pursuits like tennis, dominoes, swimming, and gardening.

I never asked my parents if they ever considered a bilingual household, but as often happened with issues connected to Cuba, I feel like I got my answer without having to ask. My gregarious, demonstrative father, Tony, was a white guy born and raised in South Carolina whose native language was not English but Southern American spoken softly with a genteel accent peppered with localisms and idiosyncrasies. My dad often characterized visits to my mom's family as expeditions to alien worlds. The presence of Spanish only seemed to underscore the outsider theme for my dad and made him feel like a fish out of water.

"You'll be lost," my dad once said to me, "but then you hear a word like *vacuum* or *Lysol*, and you know you can relax. They aren't talking about you."

But I wasn't afraid they were talking *about* me, Dad, I was sad that they weren't talking *to* me.

When I finished college, I wanted to travel widely. Never mind that I was barely making enough money from my first job to cover rent in Brooklyn, I found an airline deal to London from New York for one week. The discounted trip included a boutique hotel with daily breakfast near Victoria Station, a double-decker bus tour of London, and a coupon for two pints at Punch and Judy's. When none of my friends were available, my mother volunteered to go with me. We took five trips together, starting with London. Those trips taught me a lot about the person Carmen is outside of her identity as mother and wife. On our third trip together, we went to Spain for nearly two weeks, a trip that taught me a lot about her experience with Spanish.

Arriving in Madrid, Carmen said that Spanish in Spain sounded beautiful and proper. Great love and reverence shone in my mom's brown eyes as strong coffee melted away jetlag on that first morning. This was my mother's first language on full glorious display. But a few days in, her struggle was evident when Spaniards used an unfamiliar dialect or vocabulary. She would huff and declare it an annoyance, but I saw the frustration on her face. *I should know this, I should be better at this,* she seemed to be thinking. Yet Carmen never backed down from speaking Spanish on the trip, no matter what happened.

At lunch on our last day in Madrid, we ordered a traditional dish called *callos madrileños.* Neither one of us knew what that was, so Carmen asked the waiter to describe it. Even I caught the word *carne* in his description.

"Beef stew," my mom said and nodded to the waiter.

When the dish arrived with what looked like dead fish skin floating on top, our American stomachs recoiled in alarm. It turns out that the *carne* in *callos madrileños* is not *carne* at all but tripe. Too embarrassed to send it back, we forced down as much of it as we could.

"Drink this," my mom said after she ordered another carafe of sangría. "It will numb your stomach."

The lunchtime sangría led to a terrible case of the giggles and the hiccups, and the snobby waiter, eyes rolling disdainfully at the two crazy American women, brought *la cuenta* (the check) before we asked.

The next day on the train to Seville, she asked the train attendant where we needed to go to check our bags and blinked in confusion at his answer. I had understood enough and relayed the instructions to her. The attendant immediately said in slightly accented English, "Oh, you don't speak Spanish. Welcome aboard." *Ouch,* I thought to myself, wanting to defend my mom, *she speaks amazing Spanish, you snob, it's her first language, she just is out of practice and there's a lot of water under the bridge and . . .* I was marinating in indignation but my mom was past it, wheeling her bag to the back of the train car and ordering me to pull out the Frommer's so we could have a restaurant in mind for dinner when we arrived in Seville.

But her fluency was on her mind during the train ride. After a while, she gazed out the window at the countryside zipping by and twirled her hair like she did when she drove the school carpool. She wondered aloud about how her Spanish maybe had turned into "Spanglish." She told me that she often received emails from Abuelito in Spanish and she had to read them out loud, which makes sense since she left Cuba at the age of seven, shortly after learning how to read. She told me how she faced other people who were constantly making assumptions about her fluency. My mother spent her entire career working in hospital laboratories and drawing blood for patients, and occasionally she would be called to translate for a patient who didn't speak English. After a handful of experiences, she told the hospital to stop calling her.

"Do you understand medical English?" she asked me rhetorically, reenacting for me the moment when she had to tell the administration that she couldn't be called to translate anymore. "Medical English is a specialty. It's jargon. Medical Spanish is exactly the same thing. I do my best but . . ." Again, a sigh of frustration as she reached way back into her memories and maybe recalled the times when she herself felt lost among English speakers.

The rolling hills near Madrid gave way to the desert-like landscape of Andalusia, a province in the south of Spain famous for *paella*, sherry, classical guitar, and bullfights. For me, Andalusia was the setting of many famous works of art from the experimental film *Un Chien Andalou* to the novella *The Alchemist*. The city of Cadiz, where a branch of my Cuban ancestors originated before setting sail for the West, is a port in Andalusia. Glancing out the windows occasionally, Mom and I found ourselves laughing again about our wild encounter with tripe, wondering how *carne*, a recognizable word for beef, meant tripe in Madrid. Something as simple as ordering lunch was an adventure when you ventured out of your comfort zone.

In the ninth grade, I finally had the option to study Spanish as my mother had always promised, and I was crushed when a scheduling snafu placed me in French. Once a student was placed in a language class, that was it; French was my trajectory until I finished high school. I was devastated. How the hell would anyone ever believe that I was Cuban American if the only thing I knew how to say in Spanish was *el gato es muy gordo*?

"Maybe it wasn't meant to be," my mom said, accepting things for what they are and moving on, a lesson that I had a tough time inheriting from her. "And don't worry, you'll love French," she said like a cheerleader trying to bolster the losing high school football team through the fourth quarter.

As usual, Carmen was right. I loved learning French and I excelled. On my first trip to Quebec towards the end of high school, I dove right in and boldly ordered a cappuccino at a small café near the Chateau Frontenac. The waiter nodded and asked me a question, to which I responded, "Huh?" He winked at me and switched to English. I felt strangled by the inability to communicate, even to order coffee. In Quebec of all places, I realized that my desire to speak Spanish had not meant learning it in a classroom. I was longing for the kind of Spanish heard around the breakfast table, the kind of Spanish that comes directly from Cuba, the kind of Spanish that has a specific word for tripe, the kind of Spanish I should have inherited through the kinds of experiences that had passed before I had the chance to claim them.

During my first year in college in New York, I attended a screening of films by Cuban filmmakers, where I had one of my first encounters with Sara the Real Cuban, and my perspective on Spanish shifted dramatically.

"I'm Barbara, nice to meet you."

"I'm Sara, *mucho gusto.*"

"Where are you from?"

"Miami." *Of course.* "You?"

"South Carolina."

"Wow!" Sara the Real Cuban was beaming with excitement and curiosity. "How does a Cuban girl end up in South Carolina?"

"That's probably a better question for my mom," I said.

"*¿Habla español?* Do you speak Spanish?" No one had ever asked me the same question in two different languages before.

"No, but I wish I did," I said ruefully.

I will never forget Sara's hand on my arm and her intense gaze. I looked away but she held on to me with a firmness and a directness that was both comforting and unnerving.

"Don't be sad," she said, "I bet you know more than you think you do. What's your favorite Cuban food?"

"*Arroz con pollo,*" I said quickly.

"*Mira,* look at that! You do speak Spanish."

Interactions with Sara the Real Cuban often ended in laughter. She never, ever asked me why I didn't speak Spanish. She never used the word *shame.* She would only correct my pronunciation if I asked, which I did a lot, and she often used the bilingual approach like Grandma: "*¿Qué tal?* How are you?" She openly shared some hilarious stories, like the time she thought it would be a great idea to major in Spanish, thinking that growing up in a bilingual home would give her an advantage and she could sail through college. Listening to her speak Spanish was hypnotic. Her Spanish moved like it was in a rush to catch a train. She made the word *guacamole* into poetry, so of course, she would ace Spanish, right? *Wrong.*

A few weeks into the semester, she took a test to assess her skills in Spanish. She passed the oral exam but failed the written test. She was placed in an entry level Spanish class and kicked out of the program. The colloquial Cuban Spanish that she had used all her life didn't translate—*jajaja* (hahaha)—to the academic Spanish she needed to attain a degree. She switched majors. This story—*I took Spanish because I thought I could ace it. I failed. Oh well*—is a story that I have heard many times within my own family. Maybe it is a rite of passage for bilingual Cuban Americans to try academic Spanish and fail brilliantly. Maybe it's a good thing that I never tried to learn Spanish in the classroom. While I might have avoided tripe in Madrid, I also might have locked us out of the Airbnb in Havana.

My mom was judged for speaking Spanish and I was judged for not speaking Spanish. What my mom saw as an obstacle in her world is what I see as a loss in mine. My confusion stemmed from the belief that I didn't think anything was missing in my world until someone else told me that there was. But our challenge was the same: we were Cubans facing people who were not, who were judging us based on an ill-formed concept of what it meant to be Cuban, and who expected us to be like them and not like us. Anyone who casts shame on that has some serious soul-searching to do themselves. Watching my mom in Europe, I realized that her journey to acquire English sharpened her resilience. When she told me, "I was a kid and I learned fast," she hinted at the tough armor that she had to grow in her quest against shame. By the time I knew my mom, she was comfortable being who she was, where she was. The shamers could go to hell. If tripe stew showed up, oh well. Numb your stomach and laugh it off.

Not speaking Spanish didn't stop me from going to Cuba in 2017. Finally. If I were shut out because I didn't speak Spanish, then I probably didn't deserve to call myself Cuban. But Cuba echoed the lessons I'd learned from Sara the Real Cuban: Cuba embraces her own, language proficiency be damned. In fact, language proficiency is part of the story. How comfortable I feel in a Spanish-speaking environment, if I choose to throw out a phrase or not, even how I say *del Valle* all tell the story of my family's journey across the Straits of Florida, through the United States, to my story from South Carolina to New York. I was not shut out of experiencing Cuba because I didn't speak Spanish, and I brought back an important lesson in acceptance. I now say, "del VAH-yay" and hope to one day write a charming children's book about the farmer in the "dell valley." Who cares what is right, as long as it is mine? Who knows what is right? This is my family's name, and how I say it is the correct way to say it—no matter what—because the pronunciation makes it uniquely mine.

Sailing Around Cuba

That first night at sea, after the formal captain's dinner, I stood on the ship's deck. I was about to meet Sara the Real Cuban for the first time.

My hair whipped my face and my feet wanted to kick off the high heels borrowed from my mom. My thoughts were on the smooth coconutty taste of my first daiquiri, not geography. After a ridiculous amount of fidgeting, I finally settled and took in the expansive ocean and stars around us. Even this massive party boat with its curly slides and line dancing clubs seemed small and quiet on the edge of sea and sky.

It was 1997. My high school graduation was a few weeks away and I was on my senior trip: a seven-day cruise from Miami to New Orleans. I never would have noticed a thin strip of land dotted with orange lights off in the distance if Sara the Real Cuban hadn't pointed it out to me.

"Barbara, look, that's Cuba."

I was stunned. The cruise ship's route from Miami to Grand Cayman meant sailing around Cuba, yet I had never imagined that we would actually see it. Cuba was a mirage in the distance at this point in my life, and from the deck of the Carnival *Celebration!* with a margarita machine whirring nearby, it felt even further away, but I was now the closest to Cuba that I had ever been. Yes, I know Havana is ninety miles from Key West, but how was I actually looking at Cuba right here and now?

Seeing the island with my own eyes manifested Sara the Real Cuban for me. This was the first time I had discussed Cuba with another Cuban to whom I wasn't related. But as soon as I heard Sara's voice, I knew that sharing genes was secondary to what we did share: that thin strip of land dotted with orange lights so close but so far away. In this first manifestation, Sara the Real Cuban was both a figure of authority and a warm, down-to-earth presence. She was someone I'd known since childhood but now that I was seeing her as a Cuban woman, it was as if we were meeting for the first time. Like the women in my own family, she worked very hard but valued fun and relaxation, and that's why we were here on a cruise ship together. This trip was supposed to be a carefree pause before my classmates and I threw ourselves into the maelstrom of the graduation ceremonies and parties that would herald the end of an era for us.

But I was not getting a break; I was getting the shock of my life. After years of feeling so far away from Cuba, I suddenly found myself face to face with it.

Sara the Real Cuban half-smiled and said to me, "Yes, there it is. We are closer to Cuba now than we are to the US."

Then she told her story about leaving Cuba. Like many people who fled Castro's regime, her family was declared enemies of the state. She explained that she faced arrest if she ever set foot in Cuba, and that her family was granted asylum in the United States. I had never heard anything like this before, and it sounded horrible.

Enemies of the state? How crazy was the Castro regime in Cuba to do that? I couldn't imagine Sara the Real Cuban as enemy to anyone at all. I sailed through advanced history with flying colors in school and could rattle off some key dates related to the Cuban Revolution, but how history had affected the people I loved didn't register until that moment.

I was eleven years old, and my mom drove me to a ballet class. That summer, I was acutely aware of how we looked so much alike yet so different at the same time. Having stepped off the tennis court an hour before, my mom smelled like perspiration and tennis balls, while I smelled like WaterBabies sunscreen and chlorine after a morning at the pool. Every summer, she tanned to the shade of well-done toast, while I switched between catfish belly white and boiled lobster red with nothing in between. The daily thunderstorm brewed over the suburban tree-lined streets; the dark clouds bore a strong resemblance to my mom's thick dark hair. Also possessed by the weather, my auburn hair corkscrewed out of my half-assed attempt at a ballet bun. Stopped at a red light while B106 played Bryan Adams's song from *Robin Hood Prince of Thieves,* I noticed that my face was starting to look a lot like my mom's. I suddenly thought about how Cuban my mother looked, compared to very non-Cuban-looking me, so I asked her about Cuba.

She told me the story: in 1959, after she finished second grade in May, my grandfather drove the car onto the ferry in Havana, drove it off in Key West, and drove it all the way up the East Coast for summer vacation in Lake Placid. They never returned to Cuba. Eleven-year-old me was captivated by the idea of going on vacation and never coming back; it sounded like an amazing adventure. I remembered a photo of my grandmother with my mom and her siblings at the Statue of Liberty in 1964. Shortly after their arrival in the United States, they settled in New Jersey and started a normal suburban life, but in my eleven-year-old imagination, they had been on vacation that entire time, so long that my mother sprouted from an impish second grader into the willowy preteen in the photo. She is the third tallest in the photo after my grandmother and the Statue of Liberty.

In 1959, the family put up the appearance that they were going on vacation, but they were escaping Fidel Castro's revolution. After a short time in New Jersey, they moved to Louisiana, the place that I think of as my mother's home. My mom's forever summer vacation ended with, "and we never went back to Cuba." My aunts, my uncle, and my mother's cousins all had a similar story: they arrived in the United States and stayed for a bit, until one day their parents told them that this place was home now. One cousin, slightly younger than my mother, had apparently replied to her father, "So, I guess we can unpack those now?" referring to boxes that had been stacked in a corner of their rented Miami home for a few years.

Something about seeing Cuba from the deck of a cruise ship in 1997 made me realize there was more after "and we never went back" than unpacking boxes. Suddenly I wanted to ask my mom, "Then what?" and "How did you know to go?" and "How did you know you had to stay?" and "When did you know you weren't going back?" Over the years, the story grew more nuanced, not because there was more information to be shared but because my understanding of the world at that time changed. In my mother's limbo years between Cuba and the United States, words used to describe Cubans changed: exile, immigrant, refugee, boat person, *gusano*, enemy of the state, and other darker words depending on who was doing the labeling. But I couldn't imagine that these words applied to my family; my mother was Mom. My grandmother was Grandma. My grandfather was Abuelito. My mom's sisters and brother were my aunts and uncle. There were weddings to attend, babies being born, graduations celebrated, houses bought and sold, visits to make, holidays to celebrate, lives lived, just like everyone did. My family was too normal to have anything to do with a volatile historical event like the Cuban Revolution.

After the cruise, my mom picked me up in the school parking lot. "Did you have a great time? Was it so much fun?" she shouted above my elated teenage girl squeaks as I dragged my suitcase to the car and described snorkeling in Grand Cayman, climbing Mayan ruins in Mexico, singing karaoke off-key, and other activities encouraged by Sara the Real Cuban with a mischievous gleam in her eyes, daring me to play as hard as I had worked for my high school diploma.

A few days later, back in our routine, I told my mom that I saw Cuba from the ship. I watched her facial expression shift, and I wondered if she was struggling to remember the last time that she had seen Cuba too. She didn't know she was never going back, so maybe she never took that last look. Standing in the kitchen with the family dog licking crumbs off the floor, I had turned the tables on our mother-daughter dynamic as it related to Cuba. My mother tightly controlled her narrative—*we went on vacation and never went back . . . one day, Abuelito said this is our home now . . . and we lived happily ever after . . . THE END*—and I swallowed it, until the moment that I had seen Cuba myself. Seventeen years old, I had a new understanding as to why I didn't feel a stronger Cuban presence in my life, and I no longer wanted the sugarcoated, forever-vacation story anymore because Sara the Real Cuban told me a story that was different, darker, and more frightening. I started to see Cuba not as a faraway land from a bygone time but as a sinister place that had rejected and wounded her. My mom once told me that while she considers Cuba her birthplace, she did not consider it home. Maybe her relationship to Cuba was severed without her even realizing what was happening or marking the occasion. Maybe the sugarcoated story was for her benefit as well as for mine.

Then my mom told me what happened next, starting with, "so we got used to life in the United States." As a child now eight years old, she focused on what kids focused on: school, friends, toys, life. Their suburban home in New Jersey became a crash pad for family coming from Cuba to the United States, and my mom told me entertaining, sitcom-like tales of grandparents in the attic, bachelor uncles in the basement, an aunt's wedding in the parlor, and Abuelito shoveling snow. I laughed out loud when my mom recounted what Abuelito had said to Grandma when she asked him what she was going to do with all these people. "Give them lots of scotch," he supposedly said. That sounded like a very solid plan to me.

A few years after my trip to Cuba, my mom and I found ourselves on another trip together to see the Gilded Age mansions in Newport, Rhode Island, for a weekend during the holiday season. That train ride from New York to Providence reminded me of our train ride from Madrid to Seville where discussions of Cuba felt like a third wheel. Trains get my mom talking, and she added in some more details about leaving Cuba, details she probably only was able to add thanks to her own process of acceptance. She told me that during those chaotic years of adapting to life in the United States, she missed Cuba and worried about what would happen to her family, but she didn't know how to express it. I like to imagine Carmen, aged eight or nine, whispering to a sister, a stuffed animal, or a pillow at night, "I miss home," and I like to imagine that someone nearby responded, "So do I," but I don't think that ever happened for her.

The separation from Cuba must have only grown more pronounced as she grew up and watched as Castro's revolution rendered the place unrecognizable. Hopefully she found some solace in the realization that the choice to leave had been the right one. The end of their way of life was Castro's goal all along. Rapid changes rolled over what was familiar to her. Strangers moved into my family's homes. The Soviet Union, the supreme enemy of the world and especially the United States, flew flags from buildings in Havana that my mom would have recognized from her daily trip to school. Everything that defined their lives in Cuba had been obliterated, as if Cuba kicked them out, slammed the door in their faces, and burned the building down. Like a bad divorce, Cuba and my family parted ways and by the time I was born, no one talked about it much. Well, certain things about Cuba were fine; dominoes, yes, let's play! Help Grandma make *arroz con pollo*, definitely. But mention present-day Cuba and things didn't go so well.

When Pope John Paul II visited Cuba in 1998, staunchly Catholic Abuelito said, "The Pope is senile." Several of my mother's cousins traveled to Cuba then for the Pope's visit, no doubt very curious to be allowed entry and to see that Cuba for themselves. The biggest headline from their trip was that their mother, Grandma Faraway's sister-in-law, boldly declared that *this* Cuba was no longer *her* Cuba. When Elián Gonzálcz was returned to Cuba in 2000, I remember Carmen clearly saying, "That poor child. Why would they send him back?" The few stories I heard about family visiting Cuba also made it sound as if we tried and failed to go back: My great-uncle known simply as *Tío* (Uncle) got lost trying to find his house because the street names had changed, and on his one and only trip back in the fall of 1959, just a few months after the trip on the ferry to Key West, Abuelito returned to see what was going on in Havana. There he encountered Castro's police, who told him to leave and never return, that he was no longer welcome in this Cuba.

All of these dark stories felt like a shadow cast over me. For years I couldn't see what was casting it. Cuba was like a phantom limb that felt sensation even though nothing was there. Other Cuban Americans traveled there, supported friends and family there, and actively criticized the Castro Government. But from my family, a word or two, maybe a sentence here or there, and that was it. I was confused about the place—*You can't just buy a plane ticket and go! (Can you?) The embargo forbids it! (Doesn't it?)*—and I was confused about the people—*I don't have family there. All of my family live in the United States now. Everyone left.*

Yours stayed? Why? Aren't they starving, tortured, deprived, brainwashed, communist?

Gradually, this litany of questions transformed from a hysterical *What is going on here and how can I get a straight answer?* to *If you can go, can't I?* to *Yes, I'm going!* It wasn't just unfair, it was downright hurtful that strangers had access to and told stories about a land that was part of me. It was unfair that I knew more about Cuba from history classes, art exhibits, and *New York Times* bestsellers than from my own family or my own experience. I wasn't just missing a sense of the past; I was missing the present too. I never asked myself if going to Cuba would help me understand why my family put their homeland behind a veil; their Cuba was one from a time long ago, and I wanted to understand the role that Cuba would play in my life, today and tomorrow. I was tired of feeling unsure of, confused by, and disconnected from my Cuban heritage. So, fifty-eight years after my mother sailed away on a ferry to Key West and twenty years after I squinted at a strip of land lit by hazy orange lights in a dark sea, I landed with my husband at José Martí Airport in Havana.

My family never said to go, but my family never said don't go. Abuelito had passed away eleven years before my trip to Cuba, and I think if anyone would have come out vocally against my trip, Abuelito would have. But a few weeks before I left, my grandmother reached out. She always signed her cards and letters with "*Un beso*, Grandma." A kiss from Grandma. She sent me off to Cuba with a kiss and asked me to take a lot of photos. I was the first of her direct descendants to go. I wonder if she understood that I felt pulled towards Cuba, and I wonder if she felt the pull herself, even if it sometimes hurt. I wonder if she knew the lesson I would learn: that Cubans love their island homeland, and that the island in some mystical way loves them back.

Patron Saint of Things That Go Boom

"My name is Carmelina Barbara Caver, but I go by Barbara," I squeaked to my kindergarten class.

My names and what to do with them were too many words for my new classmates and they responded with dumbfounded blinks and stares. But my sweet Southern kindergarten teacher audibly sighed in relief and said, "Hello, Barbara," in a lilting voice. When she saw my first name *Carmelina*, unfamiliar and obviously not WASPy, her '80s perm straightened itself in panic. I had just given her an easy way out of a year of awkwardness.

Before I was born, the question of what to call me became overly complicated. Carmelina is Grandma Faraway, and Barbara is my Memah, my father's mother from Georgia. Because I was the first granddaughter for both, I was named after each of them. In my earliest memories, my parents called me Barbara and I overheard my dad once tell a neighbor that Carmelina is not a common name and it's hard for people to pronounce. Strange that they put "Carmelina Barbara" on my birth certificate instead of "Barbara Carmelina" if that was the case, but no one ever answered that question for me with much more than a shrug.

When I told my kindergarten class and teacher to call me Barbara instead of Carmelina, I parroted the words that I had heard my parents say to doctors, friends, teachers, anyone who needed to know what to call me. It wasn't strange that I went by my middle name—lots of people do—but it was strange that Carmelina came with such baggage. To me, Carmelina was never a source of embarrassment and Barbara was never a consolation prize. Together they were *my* names, unique to me and the first stepping stones with their own unique connections to Cuba.

Carmelina means orchard, garden, or vineyard of God, and you will find Carmelinas, Carmelitas, Carmelas, and Carmens in countries from Italy to Ecuador. I once heard of a town in Italy named Carmelina, and there is a Carmelina Street in Los Angeles County. The name originates in Hebrew from Elijah's mythic Mount Carmel. A Christian monastic order known as the Carmelites was founded on Mount Carmel in the twelfth century and has as its patroness the Virgin Mary under her title Our Lady of Mount Carmel with a feast day of July 16. The name Carmelina is musical, like fingers tapping over a piano; when I instruct people on how to pronounce it, their response is something like "that's such a pretty name" or "I love that name." When I hear my name, I picture not myself but my grandmother, *un poquito scotch* in her hand, resting on the shady porch at her house and surveying her garden with its bubbling fountain.

If there are parts of the world where the name Carmelina is not strange because it's the name of a local town or a main street, then there are parts of the world where the name Barbara means strange or foreign. The word *barbarian* derives from the same Latin word and in historical texts, a word that looks a lot like Barbara refers to invading Northern European tribes that brought down the Roman empire. Saint Barbara is the Catholic patroness of gunpowder, artillery, fireworks, explosions, mining, and lightning. According to sketchy legends, this strong-willed young woman defied her pagan father in the fourth century and converted to Christianity. This act of rebellion caused him to lock her in a tower, starve her, and torture her with swords. The tower was struck by lightning and burned to the ground in a terrific fire that also consumed Barbara, her father, and the swords. In Cuba, Saint Barbara is associated with Changó, the *orisha* of lightning and fire in Santería. The word *orisha* originates from the Yoruba people of southern Nigeria, and it means god or lord. The Catholic feast day for Saint Barbara is December 4, and in Cuba, December 4 is a holiday celebrating both Santa Bárbara and Changó. My name Barbara sounds guttural and heavy, carrying with it drums of invading barbarian hordes and the deep boom of cannon fire. And to put a fine point on it, I often go by its shortened version Barb which is as percussive as a grenade and conjures images of pointy barbed wire and porcupine quills.

I associated my name Carmelina with Cuba because I share it with my Cuban grandmother and, like all things Cuban in my life, it was shoved aside. I concluded that Barbara must be the most non-Cuban name ever, further proved by my grandmother Barbara. A lady through and through, she was proud of her Irish ancestry, her Southern roots, educated in Pennsylvania. She returned to the South to teach, raise her family, enjoy her friends, and watch her grandchildren grow up. Memah was the one who told me about the Latin root for our shared name.

My two names—one flowery and pretty and the other fierce and mighty—felt as if they came from two different worlds, not unlike my two grandmothers. But there was one thing that my grandmothers Carmelina and Barbara shared as a cornerstone of their personality and their lives: their strong Catholic faith. In the Catholic Church that they were raised in, the mass was celebrated in Latin, not in local languages, and every daily prayer, sacrament, and ritual down to the times to kneel during mass was universally practiced. Names are very important in Catholicism too: baptism names, godparents, confirmation names, the names of saints. When I was a kid struggling to understand why I had so much baggage around my name, I conjured a comforting vision: a young Carmelina kneeling at the communion rail of a church in Cuba, and literally at the same moment in time, a young Barbara kneeling at the communion rail of a church in Georgia. And the story of Saint Barbara was known to them; in fact, Saint Barbara connected the three of us before I even knew much about the saint herself. Often on December 4, my grandmothers called, mailed a card, or relayed via a phone call to my parents a wish for me to have a "Happy Saint Barbara's Day!" It felt like a second birthday that only the three of us celebrated. Despite the distance and difference between them, my grandmothers were in sync when it came to me.

My Catholic education from first grade until I finished high school focused on the marquee saints—"the headliners" as one of the nuns with a good sense of humor called them—and Saint Barbara was never on the bill. One morning in the fifth grade, I went to the school library and checked out a children's book about the lives of the saints. Saint Francis of Assisi (a headliner) and his story covered several highly illustrated pages, showcasing a lean Francis who looked like a shaggy-haired rock star helping the poor and playing drums in a grunge band. At the end of the book, I found Saint Barbara. Her tower prison was a thick gray block with little detail, and her face in the tower window was washed out with heavenly light from above. She was given two sentences that mentioned her virginity, her martyrdom, and her feast day. There was no mention of her connection to things that go boom, which ten-year-old me would have thought so cool, and definitely nothing at all about Changó. These sketchy details and a date in December were all I knew of Saint Barbara for twenty-seven years—until I went to Havana.

The sixteenth century Spanish fortress Castillo de los Tres Reyes Magos del Morro, or El Morro for short, boldly occupies the landscape of Havana's harbor. El Morro is the location for many of Cuba's most impactful historical events, from the Spanish colonial era to its notorious reputation as Che Guevara's prison in the 1960s. On the grounds of the fort is a well-maintained chapel to Saint Barbara, and in the chapel is a small statue of the saint in a vitrine. With gunpowder sprinkled on her red cloak and a lightning bolt crown, she appears as a strong-willed woman with literal firepower in her pockets. The night after our visit to El Morro, I noticed a mural of Changó on the courtyard wall at the restaurant where we were having dinner. The similarities were striking: Changó appeared in a red cloak with a lightning bolt crown as he materialized from a sparking thundercloud. The two images were a far cry from the faceless shy virgin trapped in a tower carefully raising her eyes towards heaven's blinding light.

I had more than a name in common with Saint Barbara's statue at El Morro; she was a short, white woman with curly auburn hair just like me, the lightning bolt crown acting as heaven-sent frizz control. But I could tell this tiny lady wasn't playing any games and suffered no fools. She was fiercely protective of her fort and more formidable than the cannonade on the ramparts. And if I was protective of anything, it was my name. If my four-year-old self spelled and pronounced "Carmelina" clearly, what was everyone else's problem? Why were there streets and towns named after the unpronounceable strange name, yet Barbara literally meant strange? Why did I have to use my middle name but my grandmother didn't? I often heard the so-called easy name of Barbara pronounced several different ways. In Spanish, Bárbara has three equally weighted syllables and soft rolling *r*'s, but in English, especially in the American South, the main event is the "Barb" and the rest of it falls off like boulders tumbling down a hill. This often causes the misspelling "Barbra," which causes my lightning bolt crown to spark in all directions. Anyone who has been unlucky enough to butcher my name gets a swift correction. After our visit to Cuba, I posted a photo of Saint Barbara's statue on Instagram with a caption explaining her as the patron saint of things that go boom, and one of my friends commented, "Well, that just sounds right."

Seeing Cuba's Saint Barbara, the first person who came to mind was my Southern grandmother, not my Cuban one. Memah was a warrior. She lived through the Great Depression and World War II. Before she married and raised six children, she went to college in Pennsylvania and worked at a New York hospital. She came from a family that valued education and wanted to pass that along to her children and grandchildren. When I moved to New York, she gave me two things: her collected works of Shakespeare dog-eared with her notes scribbled throughout and an umbrella with a pointed metal tip. *The Riverside Shakespeare* was for my cultural education and the umbrella was for self-defense.

"Carry the umbrella even if it's not raining," Memah said, "and if anyone gets close, stab them in the toe."

I never stabbed anyone in the toe, despite many opportunities and temptations, but I kept that umbrella for years and often carried it around New York when there was no rain in the forecast.

As Todd and I climbed the ramparts and took photos of eighteenth-century cannons at El Morro, I thought about my grandmother Carmelina's life and saw for the first time her warrior's journey. She faced a pivotal moment when the family left Cuba. The decision to go had always been presented to me as an easy no-brainer, but on those uneven stones with Havana's harbor spread out before me, I found a new appreciation for the difficulty Carmelina took on. Faced with an unimaginable challenge, she had to rise to the occasion. Her Havana had been one of wealth, beauty, and comfort. She was educated through college in Havana, a privilege for a woman in the early half of the twentieth century. Her experiences created a world where she expected her children and grandchildren to have as much, if not more, than she did, and not just material wealth. I witnessed firsthand Carmelina's genuine enthusiasm for the arts and education, especially music, ballet, travel, and good food. She had been a socialite in Havana running a household with servants and nannies and houses, which sounded to me like a fantastical, fairytale existence. But in the United States, she had to trade in her season tickets at the ballet and tailored hostess dresses for sensible shoes and an apron. She may have been educated but she never learned to cook, she told me once. In the matter-of-fact way that I came to identify with her and with my mother when they spoke about Cuba, she said, "So I learned how to cook. It was hard. We ate a lot of potatoes. But I learned well and I became good at it." This was a gross understatement; the Carmelina I knew was a remarkable home chef. I got my first lesson in how to make *arroz con pollo* from her one summer when she assigned me a critical job: watch the kitchen timer and keep track of how long the chicken had been simmering on the stove. Once it had been going for a few hours, she thanked me for being a good assistant and let me watch as she added a can of beer to the pot. It smelled heavenly. During our family visits to Louisiana, Carmelina was always quietly in charge, like a sheep dog herding the pack. She had a plan for the day, a plan for the food, a plan for everything. Behind the scenes she kept the wheels in motion and ran the show.

The summer between completing high school in South Carolina and starting college in New York was an exciting and terrifying time for me. *What am I getting myself into?* is scrawled throughout the pages of my diary from that summer. This see-sawing anxiety spoke to a specific issue that I faced in South Carolina. As a girl born and raised in the South, my decision to go to college in New York City was tantamount to treason. There were many people who took it as their responsibility to remind me of this in subtle, veiled ways that made it seem like they cared. Southerners are wickedly polite, and while it wasn't good manners to criticize my choice—I was going to college at a world-class university after all, not swearing my allegiance to a terrorist organization—seventeen-year-old me endured a lot of anti–New York propaganda while struggling with my own fears and apprehension. I heard everything from "the food is so expensive" to "never, ever take the subway" to "you'll come back after one year" to "it's just too dangerous" to "I can't believe your parents are letting you go" until my lightning bolt crown was on the verge of conflagration. These things hit on my own anxiety because I didn't know what to expect until I was there, and I wasted a lot of time and energy trying to tamp down the fear that these naysayers might be right. These yahoos deserved a simple "Bless your heart" (a Southernized version of a colorful expletive) but then I was too polite to respond like that. Now it would be a different story. Looking back at that time, I realize that I had been preparing for this for seventeen years: growing up in the South with a Cuban first name, I had grown accustomed to being strange and different, to going in the opposite direction from the crowd, to receiving others' incomplete and offensive assumptions, yet my biggest challenge was to not let any of this get under my skin and drive me nuts.

My grandmothers Carmelina and Barbara offered antidotes. They had both ventured into the foreign lands, both literally and figuratively, and they found inner resilience, so they understood and respected how this move was important to me. They told me that I would be *just* fine. When I told my grandmother

Barbara about someone's warning that I would be killed violently if I ever took the subway, she huffed in defiance, then she warned me not to internalize criticism and gave me a tool to deflect it. I paraphrased what she said in my diary:

"Everyone had an opinion and nothing more. You'll be the expert on New York City, not them. You will prove them wrong and they can't take being wrong. Too bad for them."

Then she armed me with the *Riverside Shakespeare* and metal-tipped umbrella, and told me a story about seeing her first opera in the rafters of the Metropolitan Opera House. "The costumes are huge so I could find the person who was singing," she said. She raved about the amazing food in New York and hoped that some of her favorite restaurants were still around for me.

I heard Carmelina's smile through the phone when she called to congratulate me. Carmelina, who had honeymooned in New York and visited often even before leaving Cuba, spoke of the so-called dangerous, homicidal, dirty city as if it were a magical place. She told me how she visited the salon at Elizabeth Arden on Fifth Avenue and walked out with a haircut so chic that Abuelito didn't recognize her. In her voice gently accented by Spanish, she told me that there is nothing more beautiful than autumn in New York. She described how the bold colors of the leaves were so stunning that it made her forget she was in the middle of the bustling city. "Walk everywhere," she commanded, "the best view of New York is from the sidewalk." Take lots of photos. She also stressed the importance of an umbrella, not as a weapon but as a device tucked elegantly into your purse to ward off cold New York drizzle. The food in New York is the best, she said, and it's my duty to splurge once in a while on a fancy, over-the-top meal, preferably with a glass of nice red wine and delicate dark chocolate. Her message was study hard, be careful, and enjoy it all. I was in my first semester when Carmelina and Abuelito came to New York for a visit, the only family aside from my parents and brother to visit me in New York that first year.

If you look at my names, or if you met my grandmothers, you would first see the difference. What is more different than Cuba from South Carolina, or Carmelina from Barbara? It is a clash of two cultures, something I experienced directly whenever someone asked, "Carm-, Cam-, uh, how do you say your name?" or whenever someone addresses an email "Dear Barbra." *(Grrrrrr)* I endured some skirmishes, but I never felt as if I were fighting a war. I wanted answers as to why one name was prioritized above the other, but ultimately it doesn't matter. When my parents signed my birth certificate, Cuba and South Carolina came together and co-existed, and I watched all my life as the two women for whom I am named demonstrated a common philosophy and approach to life. They shared more than they realized: education, food, grandchildren, me.

Now I see a mystical beauty in the similarities between them and my names. It's more than a coincidence that the name Barbara, which I always thought was not Cuban, has a mythological connection to Cuba, and that the name Carmelina, which I always thought was very strange, is common around the world. I look at my names, I think of my grandmothers, and I imagine a road with two forks: one that starts in Spain, sails southwest across the Atlantic Ocean to Cuba, pauses there for a while, turns north across the Straits of Florida and up the Eastern seaboard, and another fork that begins in Ireland, also sails southwest across the Atlantic Ocean to the South Carolina Lowcountry where it stays for a bit and moves over land to Augusta, Georgia, until it meets the line from Spain in the late twentieth century.

Cultures do not have to clash; they can twist together and support the growth and flourishing of a new branch, strong and secure in its roots. From this branch, a young woman emerged and took on a name that turns expectation on its head. The story of my names has taught me that people are layered, nuanced, and surprising; no one is what you expect. Do you really know what a Cuban American woman looks like, what her name might be, and if you think you do, why? Where and how can you and will you be surprised? Because for me, my names are full of surprises. Carmelina can be a girl born and raised in the American South, and Barbara can be an *orisha* of fire.

Flowers of the Valley

A few times a year during spring or summer break when I was a kid, my parents packed up the car with me and my brother and drove for two days from South Carolina to visit my Cuban grandparents, aunts, uncles, and cousins in Louisiana. The family homestead consisted of two locations about forty miles apart: a working cattle ranch called Valle Farm and the *L*-shaped oasis we called Grandma Faraway's house.

Behind the high brick wall concealing the secret garden, Grandma taught us how to play chess, dominoes, and solitaire. She showed us how to make homemade popsicles called *paletas*. She never did things for us; instead, she prompted us to make our beds, make our own snacks, find something to do. In the afternoon, we slipped through the hedges separating the properties to Grandma's friend's house next door for a swim in the pool which still had a diving board at a time when they were being removed for liability reasons. When we needed a break from swimming, Grandma had fruit punch and iced coffee for us. Yes, even us kids got a little coffee if we wanted it. I don't remember where the adults were; sometimes it seemed like it was only us kids and Grandma. When it was cool enough in the evening, we got in a round of croquet in the backyard. Abuelito would appear for dinner and take his place at the head of the formal dining room table. Grandma tasked me with setting the table and had me use place settings that seemed very fancy to me. Even if dinner was spaghetti or *picadillo* (Cuban shepherd's pie) or one of Grandma's other kid-friendly recipes, I laid out a set of beautiful plates and carefully arranged the forks so that it looked like they were at attention, ready for your service. I was fascinated by the multitude of ornate forks in Grandma's silver chest. My mom used her nice flatware on special occasions only, but at Grandma's, the good stuff came out every day. It was *Steel Magnolias* meets *Downton Abbey* with no sad parts.

At Valle Farm, we ran wild and shook off civilization. Valle Farm was no one's permanent residence, so everyone made it their own. In pasture four was the camphouse, home base for the family when we came to the farm. A one-bedroom hut with the tiniest of kitchens and a wraparound porch surrounded by a white plank fence straight out of *The Adventures of Tom Sawyer*, the camphouse was a cowboy crash pad, but we turned it into an ersatz palace in the bayou. Creature comforts such as a screen for the porch, a window air conditioner, and a dishwasher had been added as an afterthought. Meats were cooked outside in an oil drum with its own chimney. Every table was a picnic table. All the forks were plastic. The herd of cows would wander right up to the fence and study our shenanigans while they thoughtfully chewed and chewed and chewed. We rode horses in the wee hours when thick mist hung low over the bayou. We wore muddy cowboy boots and slept in hammocks and cots on the wraparound porch. We jumped in the back of the pickup truck to visit cows in the pasture or look for coyotes and alligators. We tossed horseshoes in the camphouse yard and hopped around the porch on a Hippity Hop with large horns and the face of Satan. It was summer camp with the extended family. It was *City Slickers* meets *Peter Pan* where everyone is a Lost Boy.

As a teenager, I learned that Valle Farm had a Cuban predecessor: *Flor del Valle*, or "valley flower." It is also a play on the family name del Valle, although we pronounced Valle Farm as "valley farm," but mostly we just called it "the farm." My mom's memories from Flor del Valle are similar to my childhood stories from Valle Farm, and one of my favorite stories of hers involves a goat. Hitched to a cart, this goat chauffeured my mom and her younger siblings all over the property. Flor del Valle's logo—a bold capital F nestled in a winged V—was passed down to Valle Farm and was featured on the farm's gates and sign on the two-lane highway in rural Louisiana. An antique iron cattle brand from Flor del Valle with the VF logo graced the fireplace lintel at the camphouse. Once my uncle and my mom's only brother took it down so my brother John and I could get a closer look; it was so heavy that it took two of us kids to hold it. I imagined the VF turning bright orange in an open fire supervised by cowboys at dawn, tall palms silhouetted against the rising sun. The logo and similarities between the two cattle ranches maybe helped to soften the hard line of "before" and "after" Cuba, but Valle Farm wasn't just an American copy of Flor del Valle; it was a special place unto itself.

My parents and brother adored the farm, but I had a love/hate relationship with it because I felt like Valle Farm was always trying to kill me. It was a test of survival for me; if I lived, I would be deemed worthy. My biggest challenges came from the punishing sun and mutant Louisiana insects. John got the lion's share of the tanning genes so I coated up with WaterBabies SPF 55 and zinc oxide at dawn and reapplied every two to three hours. Despite my militant reapplication, I still found thick red welts around the neck of my t-shirt or my ankles where clothing had slipped just enough for the sun to sear me rare. As for the bugs, they were legion. The mosquitos, fire ants, wasps, and bees at Valle Farm were supersized ravenous monstrosities rising from the bayou like Swamp Thing. I was their buffet breakfast, lunch, tea, afternoon snack, dinner, and nightcap. Despite the Deep Woods OFF! dutifully applied on top of the sunscreen in a layer so thick that I could have peeled it off in one chunk and had a mold of my own face, I still suffered from insect attacks and passed out each night drugged on Benadryl with a thick layer of Vicks VapoRub on my forehead serving no purpose except aromatherapy.

Thanks to my semi-protective patina and the general dirt-worship that we engaged in at Valle Farm, I was never completely clean. The word *bath* was used in the broadest sense and bore no resemblance to the steamy showers and soaks available at Grandma Faraway's house. At the farm, it generally meant putting on your bathing suit and using the garden hose to rinse off in the front yard of the camphouse. Extra credit was taking a bar of soap to your front yard rinse; *extra* extra credit was remembering to bring the soap back inside, otherwise a coyote might come along late at night and eat it. Coyotes love to eat soap, as Abuelito once confirmed after claiming to have spotted a coyote burping soap bubbles out in the pasture. If you rinsed in your shorts and t-shirt, then your laundry was done too. Only our jeans and boots were spared from the hose; boots were slammed against the camphouse's cinder blocks foundation to knock off the dried mud and pasture dust. The jeans, reserved for riding horses, were worn until they could walk by themselves back to Grandma's house where they were sanitized in Grandma's heavy-duty washing machine upon reentry into civilization. I remember once when a pair of my jeans was deemed unsalvageable and remained at the camphouse as an attempted offering to appease the farm gods.

Occasionally, for me, the garden hose and a bar of Ivory soap were insufficient to chisel off the buildup of sunscreen and bug spray, so a greater effort at cleanliness was called for, but that meant a near-death experience in the shower stall at the camphouse's tiny bathroom. Those were the fastest showers of my life for two reasons: first, with so many people around and only one working toilet, someone always needed the bathroom, and second, the shower curtain was a psychopathic serial killer. Innocently decorated with large orange flowers, the shower curtain was made of alien plastic likely outlawed in modern times. It was never dry but constantly weeping because the only ventilation in the bathroom was a small open window which didn't vent out the shower moisture but simply allowed in more of the swampy humidity. I quickly perfected the art of the cold shower because Louisiana for half the year is a hellish inferno and because waiting for the water to warm up meant almost certain strangulation by the wicked shower curtain.

As soon as I turned on the water, the shower curtain billowed inwards—even though there wasn't a draft—and seized me in slimy plastic. The water acted like glue and the harder I shoved the shower curtain away, the harder it stuck to me. With one hand and one foot, I fought off the shower curtain while I used the other hand to squirt Johnson & Johnson baby shampoo right on top of my head. It oozed down to break up the ponytail-shaped fossil of my hair allowing me enough time to give the shower curtain a powerful shove. While the bright yellow shampoo worked like Drano to dissolve the hair cake, I lathered up and scrubbed as fast as possible with a twisted bar of Ivory soap. Likely a casualty of too many hose rinses but yet not a coyote's midnight snack, the soap looked as if it had been excavated from Chernobyl and was likely not one bar but several twisted lumps melted and fused together. By then the hair cake was gone and the shower curtain was shedding water and circling for another pass. I rinsed quickly and imperfectly (it was actually good to leave some soap and shampoo on your person), toweled off in less than ten seconds, leapt into clean shorts and a t-shirt, re-ponytailed my wet hair, and got the hell out. All of this—bug spray, sunscreen, horseback rides, showers, garden hoses—was available to me if and only if I survived the two-day drive from South Carolina which was dicey at best. I got terribly, horribly, disgustingly car sick, and my motion sickness is the stuff of family legend. Thirty years later, John gives an epic "Barbara Puked Here" tour of every Burger King, KFC, and spots by the side of the road between South Carolina and Louisiana. With the car full of WaterBabies sunscreen, Deep Woods OFF! bug spray, Vicks VapoRub, and old blue jeans, I guess there was no room for Dramamine, which I didn't discover until I was in college and learned to my dismay that my motion sickness was not something I was going to outgrow, as I'd always been told, but that it had grown so potent that I get seasick on the Staten Island Ferry.

One hot afternoon when I was eleven, sunscreen and bug spray glued me to a rocking chair on the porch of Valle Farm's camphouse. Flies sat motionless on the sills. The breeze had the afternoon off. The ceiling fans put on a good show, but heat shimmered over the weedy front yard. The men enjoyed *siesta*, or "mandatory nap time" as one of my uncles called it. The horses were *siesta*-ing upright at the hitching post. My mom and her sisters formed a circle of aluminum chairs around a water oak to drink lemonade and chat in the shade.

"Welcome to Valle Farm, spend the night, dehydrate," I muttered to myself, wallowing in my own personal misery. It was *soooooooo* boring.

Then my two youngest aunts, Isabel and Barbara, known to all of us just as "Isa and Barbie" like "Butch Cassidy and the Sundance Kid" or "Scooby Doo and Shaggy," emerged from the house onto the porch. Isa and Barbie are children number six and seven respectively in the pecking order that starts with my mom Carmen. They are closer in age to me than to her. The summer that I was eleven, Isa and Barbie were out of college, not yet married, not yet the mothers to my set of four youngest cousins, and in charge of all the shenanigans. Armed with aluminum baking dishes, large bottles of Joy dishwashing liquid and Caro syrup, usually a key ingredient in pecan pie, and bouquets of bubble wands, they clearly were up to no good. Barbie dumped a load of bubble wands in my lap and bolted down the three cinderblock steps. I raised an eyebrow as Isa extracted me from my rocking chair with a loud suction sound.

"Come on, B," she said. "We're making homemade bubbles."

Grandma, with a huge grin and iced coffee in hand, came out to supervise. In the shade of the water oak, Barbie poured together bright yellow Joy and viscous clear Caro and directed me to stir. Isa sent John for the garden hose. All the activity piqued the curiosity of the toddler cousins who were defiantly refusing to *siesta*. My mom and her sisters nodded encouragement from the aluminum chairs, grateful that the kids were occupied. Isa demonstrated how to dip the wands in the thick Joy/Caro mix and wave them in the air. Bubbles like bike wheels rolled across the yard. Wide-eyed younger cousins squealed and took off on pudgy legs after the bubbles. I showed one toddler how to blow through a small wand and together we produced tiny orbs that perched on dandelions and monkey grass. At the fence, the cows chewed and took mental notes on the activities of the two-legged species. Boredom evaporated, the afternoon passed by, and before I knew it, a cool breeze swept bubbles across the yard as the sun dipped low. The pans full of bubble juice had turned into mud baths and it was time to hose off and grab a paper plate to serve yourself dinner.

Family visits, death-defying showers, and bloodthirsty mosquitoes faded into personal history as I entered high school. The family grew and dispersed, and the "everyone" in "let's get everyone together" started to look different. Summer vacations moved to weeks at the beach in Florida, long weekends in New Orleans, and holidays in New York, but I learned to appreciate the lessons that those summers fighting mosquitos and the shower curtain at Valle Farm gave me. First, there is a time and place for everything: croquet is for Grandma's house, cowpies are for Valle Farm. Second, WaterBabies SPF 55, Deep Woods OFF!, and Benadryl make strong armor, and Vicks VapoRub can cure anything, but for heaven's sake, don't forget the Dramamine. Third, the ability of a cow to stare for hours at anything is a superpower. Fourth and most important, never skip *siesta*.

Between leaving Flor del Valle in Cuba and establishing Valle Farm in Louisiana, my grandparents moved the family to Montclair, New Jersey, about half an hour from New York City. There is a blurry photo of my mom and her siblings in their school uniforms waiting for the bus in the snow, and everyone looks miserable. My feet get cold just looking at it. My mom often says, "You can never be too warm," as she layers up with extra socks and scarves in Colorado where she lives now. If Valle Farm tried to kill me, then winter is always trying to kill my mother, and she spends a tremendous amount of time trying to beat winter at its own game.

When Carmen was a child, winter was a very visible sign that they no longer lived in Cuba. Life had suddenly changed when she found herself ankle-deep in snow, far away from the sunbaked ranch that she never saw again. When what's familiar and comforting to you is sweating in the shade of tall palms and a goat-drawn cart, losing sensation in your toes while building a snowman in a suburban backyard pales in comparison. It took a while, but my mother finally attained the ultimate revenge against winter when she and my father retired to Colorado.

"This is how you winter," Carmen declared to me on a recent holiday trip as she adjusted her scarves and wiggled her sturdy snow-booted feet. She was sipping a steaming almond cappuccino next to a fireplace at her favorite lunch spot. Colorado in summer, however, is Carmen's playground. Hiking beautiful trails, reading on the porch in the warm sun, sipping a cool glass of chilled white wine at sunset in their backyard, she finds her peace in the great outdoors.

In my mom's Cuba, life was a balance of the formal townhouse with too many forks and the goat hitched to a cart. The itch of the starchy school uniform was washed away by the garden hose. No one cared what the forks were up to while you enjoyed a fruity *paleta* on the porch using your shirt as a napkin. I understood it well; I survived the nauseating two-day car trip by picturing the sun rising over the levee at the back of Valle Farm or by summoning the taste of Grandma's *picadillo*. Years later, the cracks in the red concrete at José Martí Airport in Havana reminded me so strongly of the cracks in the red dried mud on Valle Farm that I felt tears prick my eyelids. Of all the memories to pop up when I first saw Cuba for myself, the first one to show up was Valle Farm.

Any place with too many mowed lawns and too much snow was not going to be my family's forever home, so I can only imagine that everyone breathed a little easier when Abuelito settled his children in Louisiana and established Valle Farm. And I realize now that Cuba did not fade into history; my grandparents re-created their lifestyle not because they couldn't let Cuba go but because it was in the essence of who they were. *Flor del Valle*, when said in Spanish, makes me think of snow on droopy flowers. Transplanted to a new valley with giant mosquitos and thick, humid air, the snow melted and the flowers bloomed again. Despite mutant insect bites and peeling sunburns, I returned to school each year with tales of wide starry skies at night and alligator sightings on horseback. The horse I always rode was named Apollo, a gentle giant the size of a small elephant named for the Apollo space missions. No other kids spent summer vacations like this. Once when a college classmate assumed that my Cuban grandparents lived in Miami, I giggled at a mental image of Apollo cropping grass with his big teeth at the hitching post by the camphouse, a sharp contrast to the white sand beaches and fancy clubs of Miami.

Valle Farm was a version of Cuba specific to our family, and spending time there provided a lesson in the meaning of something more than home: sanctuary. My grandparents brought not just themselves but also their way of life and homestead from one place to another. Remembering the heavy VF logo on the cattle brand hanging over the mantle, I am aware of the irony: there was a piece of Cuba literally hanging over our heads at Valle Farm. I imagine how much they needed to root down something that felt familiar. I hope that Isa's and Barbie's kids, my youngest cousins who are now adults, too young to remember or born after Valle Farm, understand the connection to Cuba that it gave us. It is more than a great summer vacation retreat; Valle Farm and our memories of it are part of our inheritance. During the summers when I splashed and ran and vomited and scratched around Valle Farm, even if I didn't realize it at the time, I was living in a little piece of Cuba.

The Packing List

As she pulled the car into the driveway, the packing list in her head was halfway done. Zinc oxide, flip flops, bathing suits, beach bonnets, of course. Summer in Lake Placid also meant socks, sweaters, hats . . . all the warmer layers for August evenings that would feel like winter to a family from Havana. She visualized the box where seldom-used winter things were stored as she opened the car door and adjusted her sunglasses to the bright Caribbean sun.

She knew that the maid was already laundering the school uniforms to be packed away for the summer. She pictured the first day of school in Havana only four months away and a rush of unwelcome thoughts jumped into her head: Would this day actually happen? Would her children see their school again? Would the uniforms get unpacked in September? Her ability to see into the future was compromised.

Until now, the future had been easy to predict. Summers in Lake Placid, holidays at Flor del Valle, and a carefully blended mix of school, business, church, and social activities in Havana. The children would grow up, go to school, learn to ride horses, and receive First Communion. Maybe another baby would come, but the rhythms of their life were familiar and predictable. Now with uncertainty in the air, she also realized that they were very blessed.

As she carried her shopping into the house, she heard the sounds of the children playing in the nursery. The housekeeper met her at the door with a list in hand. She looked it over and nodded, thanking the housekeeper and sending her off to get started. But in her head, she kept a separate list. A list that she would never write down. It wasn't unusual to pack passports and birth certificates. After all, they were going to the United States for the summer. But it was unusual to pack wedding photos. She had decided that the morning of their departure, she would put a few of the smaller wedding photos in the pockets of her casual dresses before she closed her suitcase. She would tell the children to take a few extra toys, just one or two more than usual. Nothing that would attract attention from anyone, even the housekeeper.

No one talked about it except among family and then only with the fewest possible words, but everyone was making plans to leave. Their regularly scheduled summer sojourn to Lake Placid provided the perfect excuse to leave Havana until . . . when? Until this blew over? Until they knew more? Batista was gone and Castro was here. For now? She understood it was better to avoid any attempts to answer that question, just take the road north and hope that she didn't forget anything important. Again, her breath hitched, like a spooked horse, and she needed a beat to recover. What was important? What would they need, when, for how long, and could it be secretly packed so as not to attract attention? No one answered these questions, no one could tell her anything, she could only guess for herself.

Enough. There were things to do. But first, *un poquito scotch.*

She laid the packing list on the desk in her mind to return to tomorrow, and she went to the kitchen to speak to the cook about meals for the next few days. The shift back to a normal routine calmed her. Down the hall, the nanny was getting the children dressed for dinner. The grandfather clock chimed, and she looked at the time. Late afternoon sunlight filtering through the blinds crisscrossed on the walls, and she noticed something strange. It was May, the month of Mary, and the church bells were silent. They had never been silent before.

In the summer of 1997 when I was seventeen, I spent a lot of time imagining my grandmother packing for what would be their last summer vacation from Cuba. I was haunted by Cuba that summer, starting in late April when I saw Cuba with my own eyes from the cruise ship. I was also packing for my move from South Carolina to New York that August. From the university orientation package addressed to Carmelina, to my father's notes on the road atlas tracing a route up the East Coast that mirrored the drive my mom's family had taken so many years ago, Cuba and Cuban things were showing up that summer. Between typical summer activities like babysitting, movies with friends, ballet classes, community theater commitments, and visits to the swimming pool, I experienced flashes of the future: phone conversations with my soon-to-be roommates from California and New Jersey, the growing pile of stuff in the corner of my bedroom, and the way that stuff was so different from things I owned before, like heavy snow boots and a hunter green knee-length parka with a faux-fur hood. My mother Carmen and I were constantly making and revising lists, adding to the trunk, taking a detour to the mall to pick up something else, flipping through catalogs. It was both a completely normal summer and the weirdest summer ever. The life I knew in South Carolina waltzed with my dreams of New York; it didn't seem real that I was leaving my hometown and starting over in a strange place. I knew that summer was not just about going to college or relocating; I was changing from one *me* into another *me*. I struggled to process it and found comfort in imagining my grandmother existing in the limbo of a routine-based present and a mysterious future that can't be fully imagined.

For me, it was easy to handle the avalanche of feelings by dealing with mundane things that I took for granted, and shoes were one of these things. In South Carolina I ran around in sneakers and flip flops with specialty shoes for tennis, ballet, and special occasions like formals and holidays. New York would require different kinds of shoes for different kinds of weather and occasions, so I imagined that shoes were a big deal for Grandma as well. When you drive five children, all seven years old or younger, from Florida to New York in May expecting to stay until August, what shoes do you pack? I visualized Mary Janes, flip flops, and the 1950s equivalent of sneakers neatly tucked into a hard suitcase with metal clasps that could pinch your fingers if you weren't careful. My new snow boots were in their box, ready for the first flurries in Greenwich Village. Those boots were the biggest sign of the changes I was about to experience, and instead of panicking when I saw them, I felt strangely comforted by them. There were many things I couldn't possibly prepare for, but thanks to Carmen, snow was not one of them. My mother purchased lace-up Gore-Tex monstrosities from L.L.Bean without my input, but I knew better than to argue. My aunt Elena sent an L.L.Bean scarf and colorful wool socks as a high school graduation gift, underscoring that the Cuban overreaction to winter cannot be underestimated. Maybe there were harsh memories of cold feet in Lake Placid, many years ago but still fresh.

But there was one big difference between my packing and Grandma's: the question of how long the time away from home would be. As my mom and I packed, we knew that I would spend the next summer, or most of it, back in South Carolina before returning to New York for my second year of college. Though my mother's nightmare vision of New York City included weekly blizzards that would cause me to freeze to death walking to class on Broadway and Waverly Place, Carmen assured me that this back-and-forth would lead to a predictable rhythm for my life for at least the next four years. But, when my grandmother packed in 1959, a typical summer vacation was suddenly not typical. Did Grandma anticipate that they might never return? For Grandma Faraway, the family summer vacation was on autopilot: she handled the preparation, organizing, and packing, and Abuelito swooped in like Batman to gas up the station wagon and spirit everyone away on their adventure. The packing list probably didn't deviate much from year to year, until *that* year. Even then, Castro's coup might have only affected the packing list in my grandmother's mind. After college, when I made the powerful choice to build my life in New York, South Carolina was still there. But there came a point in my mom's childhood when their Cuba wasn't there for them to return to, the familiar was gone, her feet were cold in the snow, and maybe all they had was whatever Grandma had packed.

Questions of what was necessary swirled in my head, and I learned that my definition of "necessary" was completely different from my mom's. While Carmen purchased a comforter and blankets strong enough to survive dormitory washing machines, an electric kettle for my morning coffee, and plenty of socks for the Manhattan blizzards, I was caught in a life-or-death decision over what stuffed animals to bring. I was seventeen, still a kid in so many ways, and with one younger brother, I always had a bedroom to myself. My bedroom was my sanctuary, my mission control, my bat cave. In New York, I would share a suite of two bedrooms connected by a bathroom and closet space with four other women. Terrified to lose my sanctuary, maybe lose myself, I tried to bring some of it with me. At dawn on the day I left for New York, I stuffed the plush Mickey Mouse from our family trip to the Magic Kingdom in 1989 and the floppy

Marmaduke given to me when I was an infant into my overnight bag. Mickey with his eyes nearly worn off and Marmaduke practically flat from stuffing lost over the years were my comfort when Broadway traffic interrupted shallow sleep, when I tossed and turned with hangovers from cheap cosmopolitans, when I panicked thinking I'd lost my hearing after a night in the clubs, and scariest of all, when I had the dorm to myself accompanied only by my whirling anxious thoughts about why I had chosen this path so foreign and so far away from everything I knew. I felt strongly the tension between not wanting to go back but not knowing how to go forward, and that struggle kept me awake at night more often than the city traffic. Mickey Mouse and Marmaduke witnessed it all, bringing sanctuary to my pillow.

Did my grandmother have things like Mickey and Marmaduke smuggled in tote bags? When I was a kid, I would look around Grandma's house and try to guess what objects had been stuffed into dress pockets and suitcase linings on that trip from Cuba. As an adult, I learned that my grandparents had prepared to leave Cuba for months before their departure, that it hadn't been on autopilot, that Abuelito had been very much involved. They left as soon as my mother finished second grade and made her First Communion. Friends and relatives already in the United States had been contacted and the staff that worked for my grandparents were not only aware of the family's plans but were terribly heartbroken to see them go and worried to remain behind. During that summer, as Grandma and Abuelito enjoyed Lake Placid with their children, the question of when to return must have weighed heavily on them. In the fall of 1959, Carlos del Valle was head of the household, young, strong, many years away from becoming Abuelito. He planned a short trip back to Cuba by himself to see what was going on. On the day he arrived, he encountered Castro's police who told him at gunpoint that he no longer had a home in Cuba. For Carlos, that was the answer to his question. As the story was relayed to me, he was due to stay a few more days but instead immediately returned to the airport and boarded a flight back to the United States. The decision to leave Cuba and never return had been made.

Abuelito kept that story from his children until they were adults, and in turn, I never heard it until I was an adult. The reason why this story was never told or passed down as part of the family mythology is a mystery to me because it seems like a missed opportunity for closure. Sure, you don't tell a bunch of little kids that their father was held up at gunpoint, but I wonder why Abuelito didn't do or say something about their situation that they could understand. I imagine Carlos, in his mid-thirties, on the day he returned from that last trip to Cuba, knowing that he had seen his house, his office, and his homeland for the last time in his life.

Back safely in Lake Placid with the sun setting over the pine trees, he wrestles with the next step. Carlos sinks into an armchair and rubs his eyes, trying to rub out the memory of the gun pointed at him. He stares at his polished shoes, a reliable pair nice enough for business and comfortable enough for travel. How could he have ever imagined that these shoes would have carried him away from life-threatening danger? The creases in his suit pants and sweat stains on his shirt show not only the brief dip into Cuban heat but also the stress taking its toll. The air in Cuba had felt different to him, the familiar humidity feeling more oppressive. The fresh, cool air of Lake Placid should have offered relief but was now a sign of upheaval that he was struggling to gain some control over. *What am I going to do next?* I think that's what Carlos would have thought because that's what I would have thought, although mine would have included an expletive.

Carmelina, not yet Grandma, thirty years old, dressed in a casual sundress, brings him a scotch on the rocks. He tells her about the trip and the guns, in a matter-of-fact way that gives no hint as to the fear he must have felt. His hands don't shake the ice in his glass, but Carmelina notices that he does not make eye contact with her. He protects his Hispanic male ego, always, even when trying to carry an unbearable weight. After a few sips of scotch and a moment of resigned silence between the two of them, Carlos tells Carmelina, "Bring the children here," and he places the glass on the arm of the chair. Then Carmelina ushers four girls ages seven to three in matching sundresses and one two-year-old boy in diapers into the room. My mom Carmen, the oldest and tallest, stands at the arm of the chair and notices the ice melting in the half empty glass. Two of the younger kids climb on Carlos' lap. Another hides her face against Carmelina's legs. When he speaks, the fidgeting stops, and they all pay attention to their father. Carlos folds his hands solemnly, praying that this brings the family closure if not ease in the transition, and he says to them,

"Cuba is not our home anymore. We live here now. Home is the United States."

But no such scene ever happened.

My mother recalled how unanswered questions manifested as physical ailments as she was growing up. She told me that, after a few years in the United States, the family had traveled to Canada briefly. Upon reentry into the United States from Canada, they would earn American residency, which was required for citizenship. During the trip to Canada, my mother's fear that the family was uprooting again manifested as a severe stomach ailment. How that didn't lead Abuelito to have a frank conversation with his children escapes me, especially since the children were older. But he came from a different world and a different time, and he wasn't a man who shared much at all ever. Any insight into what made him tick had to be discerned from the people and the environment around him, and the byproducts were a stiff upper lip and aloof distance at a time when his children needed a father to guide them through a harrowing time in their young lives. Time created scar tissue over the Cuba-shaped wound so that by the time I was born, it was a thickened, desensitized patch without nerve endings.

When I was younger and looked around Grandma Faraway's house, I think I was looking for signs of Cuba and for signs of Abuelito himself. What did he cherish and what did he miss from Cuba? Just like the cattle brand at Valle Farm, one clue was hanging right over my head. Above Grandma's upright piano is a huge family tree, beautifully rendered in delicate needlepoint by Grandma herself. Centuries rendered in inches, the tree shows my grandparents, their children, their grandchildren and, most interesting to me, our ancestors. My eyes roamed over the branches starting with four-times great-grandfathers in Cuba to little old me born in Augusta, Georgia. Abuelito once gave me a tour of the tree, naming his grandfather, saying surnames like Kindelan, Macía, Mendoza. As Abuelito was pointing at María this or Luis that, his face glowed with pride and reverence as if he were gazing upon a holy relic. Like a jigsaw puzzle, pieces of my name came together from other parts of the tree to create something new. It was the first time I ever saw my name written in the Spanish tradition with my mother's maiden name tacked onto the end: *Carmelina Barbara Caver y del Valle*. All around the tree, I saw several other Barbaras, many del Valles, and of course only one other Carmelina. As her grandchildren were born, Grandma added our names in needlepoint to the tree, making it a living thing that actively chronicled our family's presence in the world. No other family that I knew traced their lineage with such detail and if they did, no one displayed it in their home as a fine piece of art handmade by their grandmother.

Another object in Grandma's house originated in Cuba and told me a lot about Carlos. A few weeks before my wedding in

2012, my grandmother called to let me know that she had sent me a gift. A day or so later, FedEx delivered a large cardboard box, and after an archaeological dig through packing peanuts and bubble wrap, I unearthed a porcelain Lladro figurine from the famous factory in Valencia, Spain. I recognized the figurine immediately from the bookshelf in the formal living room in my grandparents' house. An unspoken command forbade grandchildren from entering this part of the house unsupervised, but occasionally I sneaked in for peace and quiet, not touching anything except the floor with my bare feet and the bookshelf with my eyes. About thirteen inches tall, the figurine is that of a young woman seated on a high-backed ornate chair. Her hair is tucked under a scarf, and she wears a modest beige dress trimmed with blue flowers that sweeps over her lap and the chair. Ladylike grey slippers peek out from beneath the skirt's ruffles and her eyes are lowered towards an embroidery hoop in her lap. This woman sits very still, quietly bearing the dry desert heat and blazing sun of southern Spain, piercing the embroidery hoop over and over again.

In the enclosed note, Grandma told me something I hadn't known before: this Lladro was her gift from Abuelito on their wedding day, and she was now handing it down to me as a wedding gift. Now that it was mine and therefore touchable, my fingers slipped along the smooth porcelain as I traced the features of the focused young woman. It was surprisingly heavy, and I bicep-curled it with one hand and announced to my husband-to-be that I could take out an intruder with it. Todd insisted that we place it on my dresser in the bedroom, not anywhere near the front door where it could be weaponized.

I nicknamed it "Jacinta the Sewing Lady" when I placed it on the dresser. Jacinta and her demure eyes were silent witnesses to my grandparents' marriage and the life they hoped to have in 1950s Cuba, which I'm certain didn't include an image of their oldest granddaughter living in Queens and clocking an unlucky burglar with a porcelain figurine of a woman knitting. To me, Jacinta the Sewing Lady was both a precious and hilariously dated gift from a groom to his bride. My grandmother Carmelina does not evoke an image of a quiet lady with an embroidery hoop. She did needlepoint very well as the family tree demonstrated, she taught me how to cross-stitch and knit, but these were among her many cultivated talents. Not one thing defined her. I knew Grandma as the Pied Piper with a band of dancing grandchildren behind her. She had boundless energy that she expended riding horses, playing tennis, swimming, gardening, and walking. She was a masterful cook and skilled event planner, as even the smallest of family gatherings called for lots of logistics. And she did it all gracefully. I didn't feel as if she were bossing me around and telling me what to do, when to eat, when to go to bed, what to wear, but I did everything she told me to do. For girls like me who weren't used to seeing women in positions of authority, she was one of my earliest examples. She rarely sat down, and when she did, it was at the end of the day with a glass of wine, maybe a piece of chocolate, maybe a book, maybe her rosary. Embroidery and quilting must have been how she occupied her time when we weren't visiting, I decided.

My mother's version of her mother was quite different from mine. In Cuba, my grandmother was a society lady who left the child-rearing duties to a nanny, the cooking to a chef, and the ferrying of children to a chauffeur. While I got a hybrid of Annie Oakley and Donna Reed as my grandmother, the same woman to my mother was Queen Elizabeth II. Enigmatic, dutiful, iconic, yet distant. Maybe there are similarities between Annie Oakley and Queen Elizabeth—one is more do-it-yourself while the other has more staff—but I suspect the change in Carmelina from 1959 to 1989 was not just a geographical one. She also experienced a cultural shift moving from Cuba to the

United States, changing and evolving in a way that Jacinta the Sewing Lady in her cold, washed-out porcelain form did not. Friends who have seen Jacinta have pointed at it with a sarcastic glint in their eyes as they ask, "Barb, what the hell is *that*?" Then I explain that Jacinta is an artifact from my grandparents' Cuba, a world of chauffeurs, croquet, embroidery hoops, and armadas of silver forks. In the United States, my grandmother figured out how to be chauffeur, nanny, chef, and still get in a game of croquet, a skillset that my mother took to the next level with a career in medicine and a world-class tennis game. What I learned from Carmen and Carmelina was that the number of forks in your home matters less than the quality of the food you eat with the forks and what you've done with your time before and after you picked up the fork. To me, Jacinta is a daily reminder of Cuba and how the world changed from 1950 when my grandparents got married to 2012 when I did.

In 2017, as Todd and I strolled around the mansions of Vedado, it was easy to picture Jacinta the Sewing Lady placed in a second-story bay window of a mansion on La Rampa. I visualized the cosmopolitan Cuban world that once thrived here and saw my grandparents, looking like Hollywood golden age stars in glossy black and white stills, making the rounds at parties, hosting business contacts, attending church with immaculately dressed children in tow. It was a fairytale life, not unlike royalty, but ultimately doomed. And my mother found herself caught in a tidal shift, a revolution that may have started in Cuba with a rabble-rouser from the mountains and finished in the United States with interests and pursuits of her own beyond wife, mother, hostess. But a large portion of Carmen's childhood was spent in the limbo between 1950s Cuba and 1960s United States. The time it took for things to become predictable again was a part of her life that my mother only started to share with me when I was an adult.

On our trip to Spain, after the tripe stew in Madrid, we spent a weekend in Cordoba under the hot desert sun, just a few hours' train ride from Valencia and the Lladro factory. While we were relaxing with sangría one afternoon after a busy touristy morning, I asked her if she ever thought about visiting Cuba.

"Yes," she said to me, "I think it would be interesting to see what it's like."

I didn't pursue it with her, but I thought this sounded disconnected. Sure, Cuba was very interesting, mysterious, intriguing, forbidden, all the things that the tour books say, but Cuba was also *home*. She was born there. I had a strong connection to my birthplace and still do; though I have lived in New York much longer than I lived in South Carolina, I define myself as "a New Yorker, but I was born in South Carolina." The difference between my mom's connection to her birthplace and mine is a matter of geography and access. If I closed my eyes, pictured my elementary school in South Carolina, and clicked my heels, *poof*, I would open my eyes to find myself standing in front of the school. My elementary school is still someone's elementary school. While it is different in the present, it is not unfamiliar or unrecognizable. My mother does not think that she would have the same experience of Cuba, even though my photos of her elementary school in central Havana show that not much has changed. Even if the physical buildings survived, the spirit around them has not, and that makes the difference between my experience of Cuba and hers. The Cuba that my mother knew as home is long gone and the deep, soulful connection to home has been severed. The Cuba that my mom needed to remember traveled in boxes and in the trunk of the car up and down American highways from Key West to Lake Placid to New Jersey to Louisiana many years ago.

Jacinta the Sewing Lady quietly occupied her position on my dresser for five years, her solemn face enduring my hasty dustings, eyes demurely downcast as I whirled in her peripheral vision like the cartoon Tasmanian Devil. Until the day I returned from my trip to Cuba, and I noticed her while I was unpacking my small carry-on bag. Most of it was emptied directly into the hamper, but a few things had to be tucked back in the top dresser drawer. Suddenly it was as if I was seeing Jacinta the Sewing Lady for the first time. Noticing her smooth, bluish white hands on the embroidery hoop, I felt a strange sensation come over me, and the cold porcelain figurine came alive to act as mediator between me and Abuelito. Until then, Jacinta's presence had often made me scoff at him and dismiss him as hilariously old-fashioned: "Okay, old man, this is what you think of women," or "of all the things to bring from Cuba, you bring *this*." My twenty-first century judgment and feminist privilege faded away, and I saw a young woman seated inside a mansion in Vedado as she calmly embroiders in the hazy afternoon sun. Over her shoulder, a young man with close-cropped dark hair watches her from an arched doorway. In a lightweight suit with a pocket square, he removes his hat reverently, his dream come to life. How sad was it that life robbed him of that dream of a beautiful wife engrossed in her embroidery. I had always thought that Abuelito could be just as cold, stiff, and as frozen in time as Jacinta the Sewing Lady, but as the experience of Cuba soaked through me, my memories of him began to thaw and answers congealed around questions that had long since gone cold. He struggled to cope with how the world was changing around him, and there isn't one thing that he could have brought from Cuba or one thing he needed in the United States that could have made that struggle easier.

History and Me

There was a moment in middle school when I heard the words *Cuban Missile Crisis* for the first time. For thirteen-year-old me, who understood that my mother's family came from Cuba and whose understanding of missiles was connected to the Gulf War and Operation Desert Storm, there was momentary panic. Then I saw that my teacher had scrawled "1962" in smelly green marker next to Cuban Missile Crisis on the whiteboard, and I sighed in relief. This happened *after* my mom and her family were living in the United States. Safe in the assumption that there was zero connection between these missiles, their crisis, and my family, I slumped in my chair, flipped open a notebook, and started scribbling notes. A few weeks later, I aced the test on the Cuban Missile Crisis. I never asked my mother about it.

In 1962, she was an eleven-year-old American. The Gulf War happened when I was eleven, and what did I remember about that? Nothing much except locating Kuwait on a world map taped to the wall of my sixth-grade classroom and singing Lee Greenwood's "Proud to be an American" for the finale to the choir's spring concert. I rationalized that I couldn't expect more from my mother than I could from myself. She never was an authority on Cuba; the sources for firsthand information on

Cuba were my grandparents, whom I saw once or twice a year. I never asked my grandparents about the Cuban Missile Crisis either, but I did ask them about their daily lives and what they remembered from their lives in Cuba. They always shared; Abuelito told me about cattle drives in the hazy morning mist on Flor del Valle and Grandma talked about the beautiful beaches near her home in Havana. But their stories never sounded as if they came from a foreign country. In fact, their life in Cuba sounded a lot like their life in Louisiana: church, school, beach summers, horseback riding, *café con leche, siesta*. It seemed to me like there wasn't much more to learn until eighth-grade history when I realized that I could learn about Cuba from sources other than my mother and my grandparents. And clearly what was out there to learn was not horseback rides, coffee, and beaches.

The lesson on the Cuban Missile Crisis was sandwiched between lessons on the Korean War and JFK's assassination, not exactly a white sandy beach, *siesta*-ful time in American history. Up until then, I thought of history as a series of facts and figures to be memorized and regurgitated onto test papers, an easy A to make up for the Bs in math, something that happened to other people who had been dead for a long time. Yet with the Cuban Missile Crisis, I found myself personally connected to history with the realization that history in Cuba had irrevocably changed my mother's life and also mine. Years before I was born, history spun a web around my mother and her family, and I found myself caught in that web in my eighth-grade classroom at a small Catholic school in South Carolina. I didn't do much with this realization for quite some time; I tucked it away in the back of my mind where it sat quietly, until I began to experience history myself.

In 2001 I was living in Brooklyn. My first job out of college had me on an irregular schedule, so one Tuesday morning I wasn't due at the office until early afternoon. I was sleeping in and enjoying a few roommate-free hours. My father's voice on the answering machine woke me up to tell me that a plane had crashed into the World Trade Center. From the front windows of my apartment, I saw the top of the towers above the trees. What happened that day unfolded as the news footage and history books have recorded it, but I have my own story of 9/11. The twin towers looked like giant upright cigarette butts burning in a sandy ashtray. A dark cloud produced by the collapse of the south tower rolled over my neighborhood and hovered ominously for a few hours. When that happened, I slammed the windows shut. Day turned to night, and the throb of a headache started above my left eye. This headache has reappeared periodically throughout the years with such a distinct presentation that I refer to it as my "south tower headache." When it appears, I know I just have to ride it out. Not even Vicks VapoRub can touch it.

On 9/11, I never drank my morning coffee. I jumped up from bed to pick up my father's phone call. In my haste to open the blinds and turn on the news, I never turned on the coffee pot. Today when I turn on the coffee pot, I feel as if I have cast a protective spell over the day or set a booby trap to catch something bad. Todd and I refer to "9/11 weather" often, although now it happens in mid- or late October and not early September. Walking past construction sites in the city, Todd will occasionally say, "I smell 9/11." How the small details of my day—the coffee, the weather, a headache—took on such great significance is what I remember most.

When the wind cleared the dark clouds and the smoke from the hulking wreck of the towers streamed south over New York Harbor, I opened the windows again. The phone, a land line, started to ring. My new Nokia flip cellphone blinked all day on a fruitless search for signal. The first phone calls were my mom at work at the hospital, my roommate's father, my brother at college, then my grandmother Barbara. Blaming it on caffeine withdrawal, not earth-shattering stress, I drank water to keep the headache at bay while I listened to my grandmother Barbara reflect on the moment in her life when she learned about the Japanese attack on Pearl Harbor. A few years after 9/11, a friend expressed shock and horror that my grandmother would bring up Pearl Harbor as I was literally watching the disaster across the East River. My friend thought it was tone-deaf and could have exacerbated my stress, but I never saw it that way. In fact, for me, it was quite the opposite. My grandmother Barbara told me her story to express her understanding of what I was going through and to show me how to bear witness to these terrible events as a way to process them. She cautioned me to be patient, told me that I was undergoing a transformation, and predicted that processing this day could take my whole life.

About thirty minutes after I hung up with Barbara, my grandmother Carmelina called. My conversation with her was focused on the present, probably something that would have pleased my friend a few years later. Concerned with what my life would look like for the next few days, Carmelina wanted to know that I had enough food, water, and coffee in the apartment (and maybe a little wine?), and she wanted me to be cautious and not venture too far from home until I was sure it was safe. Most of all, in a very Carmelina moment, she told me which saints to pray to for help and strength, then she herself went to a candlelight vigil at her church in Louisiana.

In 2017, as I was preparing to go to Cuba, I came across a timeline of the Cuban Revolution. December 31, 1958. It was New Year's Eve in Havana when Fidel Castro ousted the government of Fulgencio Batista. Castro had been trying to overthrow Batista since 1953 and finally won five years later. Something about the idea of Cuban people ringing in the New Year only to have their celebrations interrupted by the news that their government had been overthrown awakened my dormant curiosity about Cuban history. Seizing upon the idea of a moment in time when everything changed, my swift-moving thoughts pivoted to my memories of 9/11, and while I remembered pretty clearly my conversation with Carmelina that day, I was surprised to realize in retrospect that Carmelina didn't draw any parallels between 9/11 and Castro's revolution. If she did, she didn't share them with me. Maybe there were no obvious parallels for her, but I saw similarities in how we both experienced the history happening right before our eyes. While we were doing normal things, a shakeup of events presented us with a choice to stay or to go. On the beautiful clear morning in September when I woke up to history, even though there was no crystal ball that clearly laid out the consequences of my choice, I decided to stay. My grandparents had no crystal ball either when they drove the car with five kids onto the ferry bound for Key West in the late spring of 1959, but they were clearly deciding to go. They knew that they were in danger if they stayed. The elite world that my grandparents inhabited in Cuba was exactly the world that Castro was attacking. As history unfolded around them, they had to leave one home behind and seek out a new home in another country.

When I went to Havana in 2017, I knew that I would see a very different version of Cuba than the one my mother and grandparents remembered. My mother never referred to Cuba as her home, just as the place she was born, and the distance that my mom had for Cuba transferred to me, whether I realized it or not. That inherited distance explained why I approached my visit to Cuba like a tourist rather than a descendant and also why I had such low expectations for finding any traces of my family's existence there. Information from my grandmother and aunt right before my trip made it clear to me that Castro had obliterated the Cuba they knew: Street names had changed, their church and school were closed, monuments to Fidel Castro and Che Guevara had replaced statues of saints and artists, and no one could quite recall locations of family homes. Even the house that my mother knew as her childhood home had more or less vanished, either repurposed as a museum or torn down; no one really knows. Of the residences that survived from 1959 to 2017, the Mendoza House did so because it was made into a fortress by the wrought iron fence around it, an island unto itself in the possession of the British Government, while history marched by on the mosaiced sidewalk. That wrought iron gate was significant for me because even though I was a direct descendant of the person who commissioned and lived in this house, I could not enter. I had to stand outside the gate.

Yet as my husband and I snapped photos through the iron bars, I realized that I didn't want to go in. I couldn't imagine this mansion as home, not in the way that I defined *home.* Home for me was a place of my own, a sanctuary for me and the partner I chose to love, a place that we painted and cleaned and maintained ourselves. The Mendoza House was a part of my history; my great-grandmother María Mendoza del Valle was a child here, and history in the form of Fidel Castro had taken it from her. But it wasn't just the Cuban Revolution that separated my great-grandmother's version of home and mine; that event might have been the catalyst for change, but nearly one hundred years, many miles of ocean and land, and immeasurable cultural upheaval in the second half of the twentieth century also meant that the life my great-grandmother lived in the Mendoza House and the life I lived in my apartment in New York look very different. The lives of the Cubans now living and working in Vedado around the Mendoza House look even more different.

Walking through Habana Vieja one morning, Todd and I came upon a jazz band in the shadow of an old Spanish mission church. We stopped for some shade and some music. The singer was a charismatic young woman in a knit cap with big sunglasses. She crooned in a rich alto backed by conga drums, two acoustic guitars, and an upright bass. Two of the band members wore shirts we couldn't miss: "THE BRONX USA" and "NYC." The song changed, and the singer's voice without a microphone rose above the instruments and carried across the populated square. Around us, everything and everyone from the tourists walking by to the garbage collectors across the street to the breeze overhead moved in sync to the music. Though we had seen pop-up street bands in New Orleans and Montreal, we had never felt so embraced by impromptu music before. It washed over us like a gentle ocean wave. The singer picked up a yellow gourd-shaped instrument and began to shake it as she moved through the crowd. I went to toss some money into the straw hat next to the drums and the singer expressed her thanks by shaking the gourd at me. I laughed out loud. The singer and the gourd danced around the corner, inviting everyone within earshot into the music. It felt so magical. It felt like no other place on earth. It felt so *cubano.*

One of the most striking things about being in Cuba was how it felt like the best things in life—music, food, art, culture, dance—appeared exactly when we needed them. Something—a savory smell from a café as we walked by, music or laughter from an open-air club, or the setting sun catching the glint of chrome on a passing car—was always drawing us in, seducing us to notice, and daring us to set aside whatever best-laid plan we thought we had. The workers painting the building across the street from the impromptu jazz band didn't miss a beat of either the music or their work. I felt this joyous rhythm in my blood; it was a stark contrast to the life I live in New York where the pace is frenetic, where my attention is always divided among seven different things, and the constant work-hard-play-hard dance frequently overwhelms me, leaving me weeping in a corner and questioning my life choices.

In Cuba both my husband and I sank easily into the cultural ebb and flow. Cuba laughed heartily when we made a plan each day only to toss the whole plan aside within moments of leaving the Airbnb. We enjoyed watching the people around us and how they blurred the lines between work and play, like paint spills across a canvas and merges into strange new colors. Probably the best thing about Cuba was the lack of internet access; once we were there, we were on a forced social media and internet detoxification, so there was no choice but to raise our eyes and take in our surroundings in ways that we never do at home. We were so shocked at how easy it was for us to shut off. Now when I find myself needing a little time off from screens and the phone, I say, "I'm going to Cuba for a bit" and I shut off my phone and electronics for five minutes, an hour, a day, whatever. "Going to Cuba" is now synonymous with unplugging and noticing the present life unfolding around you. It was a lesson in how doing without something that I took as normal could actually provide enrichment and adventure. It was a gift, not a deprivation.

But in Cuba in 2017, deprivation was everywhere for everyone else. Despite the infectious, all-encompassing joy, the realities of modern life under the Castro regime surrounded us like the streets and the buildings. The black market thrived in full view. The residence where our Airbnb was located was well kept and newly renovated, but the place next door was condemned. On the taxi ride from the airport, the driver used Spanglish to explain that he was a doctor, but he made more money in a day driving tourists to and from the airport. He offered us his card for the return trip, with great faith in my preschool Spanish and capabilities on the Cuban telephone network. The afternoon we arrived, we stopped in front of a crumbling Victorian townhouse just a few blocks from La Rampa where three young men in their late teens were selling ice cream. A small chalkboard on the sidewalk was their only advertising: *HELADO*, it screamed. *FRESA! HECHO EN CASA!* Homemade strawberry ice cream. Perfect.

An electric cord snaked from a small-wheeled cart to a generator shaking like a cartoon rocket about to blast off. Clouds of cold air escaped from the opened cart as one of the guys scooped out the ice cream studded with chunks of strawberry and smashed it into sugar cones. I handed over three Cuban convertible dollars, even though the price we had been quoted was two dollars. The youngest of the three handed me change and I waved it away, intending to leave it as a tip. About a block away, we were lost in our ice cream cones and barely heard urgent footsteps behind us. We turned to see the youngest guy running up to us with my dollar. He handed it back to me and the meaning I gleaned from his flood of Spanish was that we had overpaid. I didn't have the words to explain that it was a tip, so we just thanked him for returning it and went on our way. A day or so later, I dropped the dollar in the street band's hat.

In a country with two currencies—one for locals and one for tourists—where doctors make more money driving taxis than practicing medicine, both Todd and I found the entire interaction with the self-employed ice cream vendors amusing and strange. Why the guys wouldn't keep a dollar that I had clearly left for them was baffling to us; had the roles been reversed, we would have had no qualms at all about pocketing the extra dollar, especially if we knew it would buy a few extra eggs or an extra quart of milk or a little more beer from the black market. This was our first experience of the kind of commerce that many Cubans participated in, the kind that thwarted the communist system of rations, shortages, and not-entirely-privately-owned businesses without going too far. The Cuban people were masters of managing: They managed empty shelves, goods available for exorbitant prices, and cars that looked pristinely vintage but were pieced together like Frankenstein from whatever working parts could be found. More interaction with tourists meant more tourist currency in local pockets. At our Airbnb, the cost of breakfast was a steal, but for Maddy and her family, it meant more food of better quality. Two slices of ham on our plate, four on hers seemed a worthy cause to put my dollars towards. Her charming daughters, ages six and eight, told me how much they loved visitors in *el Airbnb* because it meant that there was *pan de chocolate*. This was how we learned that *pan de chocolate* was different from the French sweet that we were familiar with; the Cuban version was a perfectly round roll of fluffy bread covered in a thin dark chocolate shell. It was so delicious that I captured it forever in a beautiful photo. Through her Airbnb business, our host managed a livelihood for her family that was a cut above what the government provided. And it seemed to me like everyone in Cuba was figuring out some way to do just that.

Abuelito was a contemporary of Fidel Castro. They attended university at the same time, where Castro's reputation preceded him. Once, and only once, I heard my grandfather talk about Fidel Castro, and because Abuelito was speaking Spanish, most of it went over my head, except for one word in English: *OBNOXIOUS*. Just like that, in all caps. His angry tirade echoed in my head as we walked around Havana, and I found myself asking questions tucked away in dark corners for years, questions that were obnoxious enough to defy answers:

If my mother's Cuba was a culturally vibrant country, why did Castro have to mess it up?

But . . . my mother's Cuba was also a society rigidly divided by class and governed by corrupt dictators, so how long was that really going to last?

What about the American involvement in Cuba after the end of the Spanish–American War?

What about my ancestors that came from Spain in 1550-whatever?

Why has the embargo gone on so long?

How far back does all of this go, and how much longer do we have to endure this?

Whose fault *is* this?

And history—in the form of a revolution on an island in the middle of an ocean twenty years before I was born—smacked into me like a freight train. The events of the past impacted how I learned to relate to a heritage that had eluded me. There was a full moon over the Malecón on the night that I decided I needed to let history be. I gave up trying to answer the questions posed by history, and I sent a rueful "good luck" towards the historians and future inhabitants of this world who would attempt to tackle that task. I boarded the JetBlue flight back to New York City's JFK airport (*JFK . . . ah yeah, he had a role in this whole mess too, didn't he?*), and I threw all of my questions into Havana's deep harbor to sink except for one: *what can I do, now that I know what I know?*

When I look at my photo of the *pan de chocolate*, which I often do, I remember Maddy, our Airbnb host, and I wonder what separates her life from mine. It oversimplifies things to say it's a matter of geography; it is much more than that, but sometimes I think there are more similarities than differences. Aren't we both two women in our forties trying to make the best life possible for ourselves and our loved ones? Yes and no. For me at home in New York, having a *pan de chocolate* is as simple as walking down the street to the bakery; for her, it's a calculated act that carries a pinch of defiance, a middle finger to the obnoxious dictator and his family who have been in power for as long as she can remember. There are things that I do without thinking twice, but Maddy has to play her hand a lot closer to the chest and keep an eye on the mercurial temperature of the government, who most of the time look the other way when it comes to the black market and tourist dollars that escape official channels. But when the Cuban Government wants to control something, then control it they do. In the years since my trip, this has become more obvious to me as the restrictions on internet usage loosened and many Cuban artists, writers, musicians, filmmakers, and journalists took to social media. They bravely used the platforms to tell the world their side of the story, and in 2021, social media contributed to a series of historic protests in Cuba against the government. Thanks to Instagram and Facebook, I watched along with the world as it unfolded.

The COVID-19 pandemic in Cuba strangled the tourist industry and shed light on the regime's ineptitude to distribute resources and manage a crisis. Economic collapse, widespread power outages, and shortages of food and medical supplies became the latest in an exhaustive list of the regime's transgressions going back many decades. Thousands of Cubans risked their lives to join protests across the country and call for an end to communism and the resignation of President Miguel Díaz-Canel, the Castros' puppet. It was both a cry for help in the face of a humanitarian crisis and a bold plea for social and economic change, and it was completely unprecedented—and not in a stockpile-the-toilet-paper, everyone-work-from-home way.

I first heard about the protests through social media, and then Sara the Real Cuban and I hopped on a Zoom call and she told me about what her family in Cuba was going through. After months of being unable to send food, money, and supplies to her family, she told me that they had lost contact. Some of her Cuban family had contracted COVID and no one knew if they were alive, severely ill, or dead. She was one of many Cuban Americans who reached out to the White House and to her representatives in Congress with a plea to roll back the embargo's restrictions in light of the dire situation, but she worried that their pleas for the United States to intervene in Cuba fell on deaf ears. And she was right. My heart broke for her and her family and so many others like them; the limbo that they all found themselves in was deadly and unnecessary. And my heart broke for my family; sixty years ago, they left to avoid this level of oppression and fear. Each person out on the streets risked their lives to speak out against their government. I made myself both a witness to the history that the Cuban people found themselves in and a fervent supporter who was cheering them on and praying for their safety from two viruses: the government and the delta variant. I know in my bones that no one—not my mom, not Maddy, not Sara the Real Cuban, not the artists and scholars who have been detained, tortured, and killed—deserves to suffer the effects of the Castro regime. In 1959, my family was lucky enough to have the ways and means to escape, but it came at a high price for all of us, including me as I struggle to understand my heritage. Was the world of the Mendoza House doomed to pass away and change forever? Yes. Did it have to give way to Fidel Castro's Cuba and the United States embargo? I wish it hadn't, but that doesn't mean it has to stay that way.

If I sound idealistic, it is because I cannot approach Cuban politics rationally, not after having been there and placing that missing piece into my puzzle. I struggle with feeling that I just don't know enough, but then I come back to Abuelito's assessment of Castro as obnoxious. It more than resonates; I agree. There always seems to be more to read or another perspective to understand, both politically and emotionally, so I have started. Little by little, I step into the community. I tell people that I am Cuban American, and I try to read everything I can and listen to anyone who wants to share their experiences with me. I am trying to connect with Cuba wherever I can find it.

The González de Mendoza Family is one of the largest Cuban American families in the United States with over two thousand living descendants. The most recent in-person reunion in 2021, while Cubans were taking to the streets of Havana to risk their lives in protest of their government's injustices, brought together 850 Mendoza descendants. Additionally, the family publishes the *Descendants Book* which lists the entire lineage dating back to the family's origins in Spain.

I don't need a DNA test to confirm my roots; I appear on page 237 of the 2022 edition of the *Descendants Book.* In the current edition's foreword, Pablo G. Mendoza notes that for future generations, "there will come a time that it will be possible to have this reunion in Cuba." He challenges the future generations to "take us back home!!" Any hope of change is on me and my generation to redo, rebuild, and reconnect. Some days it feels like a faraway dream, and some days, it feels like maybe in my lifetime, maybe in a few years, a bunch of descendants like me will be able to go, but I can tell my family members that it won't be going "back." We can't return to the past, but we can look at the present with open eyes and say honestly, "Here I am. *Listo*, I'm ready. *Vámanos*, let's go."

She Who Builds a Church

The graceful spires of la Iglesia del Sagrada Corazón del Jesús rise above the former Reina Street in central Havana. The first stone for this Jesuit church was laid on August 7, 1914, and it is one of the must-see architectural sights in Havana. For me, it also holds a trove of family history. My great-great grandparents contributed to the church's construction, my grandparents celebrated their wedding there, and my mom attended the school. An article appearing in the English edition of the *Havana Times* in 2011 mentions my great-great grandparents Francisca Grau and Francisco del Valle as two of the "four wealthy Havana families" who were the church's principal donors. Francisca is the only woman listed with her maiden name, separately from her husband, so to me it looked like Francisca was the only woman in Cuba with the power to raise a church.

Todd and I stopped by Sagrada Corazón (Sacred Heart) on a Sunday afternoon. Leaving behind the cruise ships and the photo-op streets of the old colonial quarter, we slogged through the heat and hustle of modern Havana. It was like Manhattan during rush hour in mid-August. Unlike Midtown's dichotomy of sleek glass towers, elegant mansions, and cacophonous traffic, central Havana was a chaotic mess of crumbling edifices, half-baked new construction, mule carts, smoke-belching trucks, and crowds. Choking on the mid-afternoon smog, we considered hailing a 1950s-era taxi—identified by the cardboard "TAXI" sign pasted to the dashboard—to jolt us back to the rumbling yet effective air conditioner and mini fridge of cold beer in Vedado, but we pressed on. Then the church's spire rose overhead, and cool air whooshed across our faces.

I stared up at the towering spire and remembered two black-and-white photographs from albums with yellowing pages: one, a stately image of my grandparents, wed for a total of thirty minutes, walking with linked arms down the aisle, and two, a solemn portrait of my mother, age seven, kneeling at the communion rail. White veil perched on her head and prayer hands folded for the photo, my mom's childish face was a blend of Mona Lisa-like smile and sneer. The setting for both photos was the interior of the church in front of me and the subject of both photos was foundation: my grandparents starting a new life together in marriage, and my mother starting her journey in the Catholic faith with the sacrament of First Communion. But I couldn't go inside the church on the day I visited because it was locked. I was extra pissed off by the idea of a locked church, since faith is supposed to be all-encompassing, as I pushed uselessly on the heavy doors. Being locked out of all things Cuban was the story of my life, and being locked out of a church in Cuba that my family built felt like retribution for a lifetime of struggling with an inherited religion that I never fully embraced.

In the shadows of Sacred Heart in Havana, I remembered another hot day; this time, I was in Augusta, Georgia, and my brother and I, ages twelve and fourteen respectively, buckled ourselves into the backseat of my grandparents' car. A few days earlier, one of my mother's cousins was married in Augusta, about an hour away from our home in South Carolina, and my Cuban grandparents had driven from Louisiana for the occasion. After the wedding weekend ended, my parents handed off my brother, me, and our small suitcases to our grandparents for a long fourteen-hour drive back to Louisiana, where we would spend two weeks that summer with Grandma, Abuelito, the horses at Valle Farm, and the chess set at Grandma Faraway's house. My parents, looking forward to some child-free time, waved a hasty bye-bye and sped away with alacrity. My brother and I waved back, prepared for the long drive that would end in two weeks of horseback riding, swimming, *arroz con pollo*, and other shenanigans. We were excited to have our grandparents and all the Valle Farm fun to ourselves for a bit. The last thing on our minds were the two rosaries that Grandma handed to us from her position in the passenger seat.

"Before we put on our music," she said, referring to our portable Walkman cassette players with foam-covered earphones that we held in our laps with cassettes clicked into place, "we are going to say a rosary for a safe trip and a wonderful visit."

Headphones bungee jumped from our heads as my brother and I each obediently took a set of rosary beads. My brother's eyes shouted an expletive but given my legendary motion sickness, prayer seemed like a good idea, or so I thought as I rubbed the beads of the rosary between my fingers. At fourteen, I was competing for lots of titles and recognition, but "World's Best Catholic" was not one of them. When it came to being Catholic, I didn't get the love and salvation message; I got the penance and unworthiness message. To me, prayer meant begging the heavenly hosts to improve me because I wasn't good enough. Every perceived flaw, from motion sickness to struggles in sixth grade math to my legs being deemed too muscular for ballet to having a high-pitched squeaky voice, were moral failures. Sometimes it felt like the sin I was atoning for was that of existing in the first place. I couldn't sense God through the pervasive anxiety bubbling in my soul. But as a child and preteen, I couldn't articulate this to myself, so my worries assumed the form of questions. *Lots* of questions. Questions that I rarely felt brave enough to ask, so in addition to having too many questions, I had too few answers and a long list of things that made no sense.

At the top of the list of Catholic things that made no sense was God with a capital *G*. If God was supposed to be a benevolent, loving father, why did he let Romans brutally murder his only son? Churches didn't make any sense; if God was omniscient and present everywhere, then why was it only acceptable to worship inside the four walls of a church? Sacraments made no sense; there are seven in total but most people only receive six if they are lucky, and why are certain sacraments so special that they only happen once, like Baptism, while others happen over and over, like Communion and Confession? My grandmother Barbara bragged about receiving Last Rites several times, which you should probably only get once since it's the one you're supposed to get before you die. Death made sense but the whole pageantry around it didn't. If death means we're moving on to spend eternity in heaven with God and his saint club, then why are funerals so sad? For that matter, why is sadness such a hard thing to understand, made worse by the fact that everyone tells you to pray or "give it to God" and no one actually talks to you about it or tries to help you feel better? Priests didn't make any sense at all; how is an old man who isn't married and doesn't have children supposed to teach me anything at all about life? And I'm supposed to confess my sins to this creep? Are you kidding me? *My sins*? My deepest, darkest, scariest moments? I'd rather take my chance with Satan and the coal in hell that supposedly has my name chiseled on it and grows hotter with every sin I commit. By the way, if sins dirtied your soul and confession washed it clean, then what is a soul, exactly? Is it a washcloth? A quick dry shirt? And why did my soul feel renewed and rejuvenated, not dirty and tarnished, after the times I broke a commandment with a lie to my mom about a headache so I would be excused from school to nurse my fake headache at home reading Nancy Drew books all day?

Only one thing made sense to me: the rosary. To start with, it was portable. My dad once told me that he prayed the rosary while he was out for his morning run. I prayed the rosary often in my room or while soaking in the bathtub. A set of prayers tracked on linked beads said to the Virgin Mary asking for her intercession to God on my behalf, the rosary made sense because it was a direct line to the Virgin Mary, priest not required. I couldn't talk to God directly, so it was great that Mary wanted to do it. She exhibited superhero tendencies, the most obvious being that she was both a virgin and a mother. She had many disguises and specific powers: Our Lady of Lourdes has a healing spring that cures everything from hangnails to cancer, Our Lady of Guadalupe crushes snakes with her bare feet, Our Lady of Fatima commands the sun to dance, and there are many more. Now here was a being in whom I could place my faith, my woes, and my love, and I felt that she would stand by me, listen to me, and best of all, not judge me. I couldn't feel God in my soul, but I could feel gratitude to this amazing lady, this Wonder Woman/Super Mother in her blue veil, this female Navy SEAL of the Catholic Church who parachuted in for every crisis I had, dealing with the weird and scary stuff while crushing snakes and dancing with the sun. Most of all, these early conversations with Mary through the rosary helped me find my inner fortitude to be myself and to be secure in my choices while facing whatever challenges the outside world wanted to throw my way.

When Grandma handed me the rosary beads from the glove box, she was handing me the only Catholic practice that held real meaning for me. We were sending up the Bat Signal, and I believed that the Virgin Mary, Holy Mary Mother of God who prayed for us sinners, would respond. We might not see her benevolent hand gracefully moving the car away from hideous pileups and redirecting violent summer storms, but arriving safely in Louisiana fourteen hours later was proof that Mary Full of Grace had protected us. As our fingers counted the beads, our mouths spoke the prayers. Exempt from holding the beads because he was driving, Abuelito recited the words in a practiced cadence as he flipped on the left turn signal and merged the car onto the highway. My brother and I were keeping pace, the words flowing together in a drone, while watching the Georgia countryside roll by. For an outsider looking in, we probably looked like robots with flapping lips, not like a family uniting in prayer for security and safety. To me, the actual words of the prayers were secondary to my intention. The words were just the code, like the Batphone or the password to the secret door in the labyrinth, a prescription handed down over the centuries that was used to contact the Virgin Mary specifically and not Jesus, one of the other saints, or crazy old God. But while my voice was on autopilot, my thoughts were begging, pleading, bargaining:

Hello, Virgin Mary, Superhero, pleasepleasepleaseplease don't let me get carsick. My brother will laugh at me. It's humiliating. Pleasepleasepleaseplease strengthen my stomach. If you do, I'll never cuss again.

I looked up from my frantic bargaining to see Grandma in the passenger seat and my rote speech stuttered. Her head was not bowed. Her fingers did not squash the rosary beads to a pulp. Her eyes were not squeezed shut. She spoke the same words in rhythm with us, but she was saying each word carefully and delicately as if discovering it for the first time. She looked out the front window with the highway expanding before her, and she was seeing the trees, the other cars, the gathering clouds, the world around her. To look at her during the rosary was to see a woman fully immersed in a simultaneous experience of prayer and life. And it was obvious to me that Grandma was in her happy place, her touchstone of peace and stability. When we finished the rosary, Grandma sighed contentedly, a sigh that was her transition out of prayer. Then she collected the beads from us and tucked them lovingly in the glove box. As if nothing extraordinary had happened, she switched on NPR while Abuelito drove us west. In the backseat my brother and I put on our headphones, but the vision of Grandma praying had seared itself into my memory.

So THAT is what praying is, I remember thinking.

Ten hours later, my stomach churned as I rinsed out my mouth in a gas station bathroom just over the Mississippi-Louisiana border. I thought to myself, *damn*. Whatever I had done, it clearly wasn't praying.

The Catholic Church sets aside certain days as Holy Days of Obligation, and obligation was how my parents, brother, and I practiced our faith. Sure, we attended weekly masses, even when traveling and on vacation. We attended Catholic schools. I sang in the choir, my brother was an altar boy, and my parents maintained their membership on the church roster, but ultimately attending church felt like an obligation, and this coming from a kid whose greatest joy was to take the dog on long quiet walks through our hilly subdivision. When it came to church, what sparked joy was the fun we could poke at it. We conspired among ourselves to perform as few obligations as possible and stay in good standing as Catholics. It was an inside joke that we all shared, as if religion was a coffee shop that gave you every tenth coffee for free. For us, faith was more about staying out of hell than getting into heaven, and each week we tried to check off our Catholic to-do list as fast as possible and negotiate ways to get ahead:

"Does so-and-so's wedding count for this weekend's mass or do we have to go again?"

"I confessed my sins to the dog and God hears everything."

"I will show you sin. Vegetarian pizza. That's a sin."

"Why don't you do some penance in advance and rake the yard?"

"The school mass counts twice because half of it is in Latin which is way harder than English."

A summer or two before my brother and I traveled without our parents to Louisiana, my family's casual attitude towards Catholicism clashed radically with Abuelito's. The extended family had gathered at Valle Farm for summer vacation as usual. I came up the cinder block steps of the camphouse, stomped my cowboy boots on the porch's wooden floor, and crossed the threshold into the camphouse's main room, which was a combination of a kitchen, living room, sunroom and dormitory. The heels of my boots stopped short. As I often did, I was interrupting a conversation among adults with a capital *A,* so I waited a beat for someone to shoo me away, but that didn't happen. I had walked into not a conversation among adults but a Wild West showdown. On my left stood Abuelito, ramrod straight in his checkered farm shirt and jeans, eyes blazing in fury. On my right was everyone else—my parents, aunts, uncles. Abuelito looked ready to fight everyone. I was completely frozen in space and also totally invisible to everyone in the room. I openly listened to Abuelito as he interrogated the other adults about how they practiced their faith.

Question: How often did we attend church?

Answer: The bare minimum requirement for it to count. (My father answered that one, of course.)

Question: What did we wear at church?

Answer: Soccer uniforms, tennis clothes, sweatpants over a ballet leotard, it all depended on when we could get to church depending on whatever else we had going on that day. (If anyone had asked me, I would have added that what you wore didn't matter thanks to the choir robe. Toss it over anything, keep your footwear modest, and *Gloria in excelsis Deo* for all the Catholic credit you could get.)

Question: Do you pay attention to the readings and the homilies?

Answer: What, and miss nap time? It's not like there's a quiz after church. Besides, I have to save my brain power for school. Don't ask me to count fishes and loaves—I'm still praying rosaries to Our Lady of Algebra II.

Abuelito was increasingly displeased and infuriated with each answer. When shame and threats of eternal damnation didn't work—to this day, I marvel at the skillful way in which my parents, aunts, and uncles deflected shame like teenage mutant ninja turtles—Abuelito then noticed me, standing in the doorway barely hiding my giggles. He barked at me to round up the children. As we marched in, he asked everyone present, from the youngest toddler on up, when was the last time that he or she had attended confession. The room got quiet as one by one, the reply was similar: "I don't remember."

Uh-oh.

Then Abuelito roared, "*VÁMANOS!*" Off we went in four cars and two trucks to a Sunday evening mass at the church closest to Valle Farm. This was not the usual church that we attended in town, a few blocks from Grandma's civilized garden and croquet pitch, where formal church attire like neckties and stockings were the unspoken dress code. This was a small country church next to a bayou where jeans and cowboy boots were formal attire. As I picked caked mud off the cuffs of my jeans on the way to church, I considered how this was proving my point about church attire. *Did it matter what we were wearing as long as we were there*? I wanted to ask but knew better.

After we had all received the sacrament of confession from a human priest—no, *el perro* did *not* count, *ay!*—we found ourselves trapped in the front two rows of the un-airconditioned church halfway through the longest sermon ever. Even Jesus was bored. I was one of Dali's melted clocks oozing onto a pew that was brand new during the Inquisition. The priest's voice was a fly buzzing around my head that could not be swatted or sprayed with Deep Woods OFF! Probably egged on by Abuelito himself, the priest descended from the altar, arms spread wide and priestly garb fanned out like a net to catch the wicked and deliver us to grace. He stood facing the pew where we were all seated with our spanking clean souls and dirty jeans while delivering his homily. The monotone bore into our heathen skulls. I had no fear of going to hell; I was pretty sure we were already there.

Then out of nowhere, Grandma said to the priest, "Santa Mónica."

I hadn't heard the priest's question—no one had—but it was safe to assume that she was not talking about the California town with the famous pier. While I was tallying my suffering to cash in later—one for each drip of sweat down my spine, two for each exasperated sigh I didn't make—my grandmother was in her element. I don't think she cared whether we were there or not. In fact, that was the first time I had noticed her during the whole fiasco. She was leaving it to God and Abuelito to sort us heathens out. She later replayed the entire homily for us about Saint Augustine and his high-rolling playboy life in pagan times. The priest had asked for the name of the mother of Saint Augustine, and Grandma nailed it for ten get-out-of-hell-free points. In a powerful story of maternal love, as Grandma explained to us later that night, Saint Mónica's steadfast devotion to faith and prayer caused her son to repent and convert to Christianity. Hmm, not unlike Abuelito was trying to get his shame-proof progeny to repent our wicked ways and not treat church like an errand to squeeze between basketball practice and so-and-so's birthday party?

In their actions that day, my Cuban grandparents lived out two versions of faith: Abuelito acted as patriarch, taking his authority directly from God with a capital *G*, hoping to save our souls through ritual and lessons, and Grandma practiced what she believed not out of obligation but out of joy, love, and faith. Grandma's example in the stifling rural church that day affected me more than Abuelito's; he may have intended to make us better Catholics, but the opposite happened. The very next week back home in South Carolina, I am sure I wore sneakers or maybe even a bathing suit under the choir robe. I quit choir after eighth grade, and by the time I was in college, out of the house, and on my own schedule, I still went to church each week but only participated if I needed something from the heavenly hosts. I showed up late and left early if there was something more interesting to do. I still prayed the rosary on occasion, but I never went to confession again.

Nearly twenty-four years after I melted in the nave of a rural Louisiana church, I found myself melting on the streets of Havana, locked out of my family's church. I thought of my grandparents, Abuelito who passed away in 2006 and Grandma who I would characterize as a daily churchgoer, and how much their faith was a foundation of their lives in Cuba. There was a lot they couldn't bring with them to the United States, but their faith was part of them. While my grandparents were taking my mom and her siblings to church in New Jersey in the early 1960s, Catholics in Cuba were being arrested for doing exactly the same thing. When Fidel Castro came to power, he actively persecuted Catholics and forced the church underground. I have no doubt that Grandma and Abuelito would have practiced their faith underground, but when I thought about what I would do, I can't say that I would have done the same thing. If

I'd been living in Cuba in 1961 and found the church locked, I would have done exactly what I did in 2017: turned around and walked away.

Under the spires of the church my great-grandparents built, I finally forgave myself for not being a good Catholic. The Inquisition-era pews, the threats of hellfire and brimstone, and absolution from the dog had not made me a better Catholic. While my grandparents attended mass regularly, I often found myself wide awake after I'd prayed the rosary wondering if anyone was listening. Some people would say that I did well in advanced math like calculus because of all those rosaries said to Our Lady of the Graphic Calculator, but I attributed it to one good math teacher who told me to stop praying and start studying. It's probably worth mentioning that this math teacher was also a nun. Were my prayers answered, or was I just growing up? Rather than running away from my flaws, I challenged myself to get to know myself better. I decided to stop trying to conform myself to an idealized version of a person I didn't think I could be. I didn't need to be absolved of sin, thank you very much, I just needed space to be me. Living a life without faith in something bigger than myself seemed like casting off to sea in a tiny boat and hoping a monster didn't swallow me whole, but living a life within the human construct known as the Catholic Church, or any organized religion for that matter, felt as if the life was being sucked out of me, sliced away not by something that brought real pain but by something that stung little by little. Death sliced as thin as a communion wafer.

Slowly, other practices replaced guilt-fueled church attendance and coldhearted, unfeeling prayers that too closely resembled frantic bargaining. I have religiously kept a diary since the age of nine, and those pages are my own little private Gospel According to Barb. In college, my writing practice expanded from private musings, personal scribbling, crazy wild daydreaming, and vengeance prose into short stories, screenplays, novels, and eventually the nonfiction odyssey you're reading now. I skipped church on Sundays and instead took yoga classes and long walks in New York City with occasional stops at cafés and park benches for journaling, staring into space, and lots of crying. New York City is the best place in the world to cry yourself out. Just let the tears flow and watch them run into the gutters and out to the East River where some barnacle growing on a sunken subway car will slurp them up. After a bit, I always started to feel better, and problems solved themselves if I could just sit quietly with my thoughts and be patient. At some point my tears washed my Catholic card into the gutters too, but it took me a few years to notice. I started to find Our Lady of the Superpowers in the gym, in the office, on the subway, anywhere that a physical or mental challenge called on a deep reservoir of mental fortitude. Call it praying, call it mantra, call it self-reflection, call it self-care. Naming the action doesn't matter to me. What matters is the peace and the strength that it brings me, strong enough to raise a tall spire, visible for generations to come, able to withstand persecution, tyranny, and despots, no matter what form these enemies take. Our Lady of the Superpowers has a new lair, and it's located deep inside my soul. A slow inhale can take me to her wellspring of benevolence more real and tangible than any hard pew or uncomfortable pair of sweaty dress shoes could ever do.

Seeking La Coronela

Miramar. Vedado. Habana Vieja.

Before my trip to Havana, I didn't know what these words meant, but after, they came to life for me, and my real-life memories replaced photos and film clips. These are the names of places that bore my family's footprints. Miramar is a beautiful seaside suburb west of Havana where my grandmother grew up, and Vedado, where my grandfather's family had several residences, is the cosmopolitan capital of Havana. Habana Vieja is the oldest part of Havana, dating from the early Spanish conquistador era, where my ancestors from Spain would have started their lives in thc New World.

My aunt Elena had a career as a travel agent, and I thought that made her one of the coolest people I knew. Her adventures to places like China and the Balkans captured my imagination, and she kindled in me the desire to travel far and wide and come back with stories to tell. She was a tour book personified: "While you're doing your internship in Cannes, take a day trip to Saint Paul de Vence. You can have a *café creme* at the Café de la Place and watch the old men play *petanque* for an afternoon. Or you can pick up some fresh bread, cheese, and fruit from the local markets and find a quiet courtyard to settle in for a lovely lunch."

About Habana Vieja, my aunt said, "There is so much architecture from the Spanish colonial era, even up until the Victorian Age and Art Deco. Take your camera and go without an agenda. You'll have so much fun!"

She was right, of course; my husband and I found some great bars in Habana Vieja run by British expats with cheap beer, great food, and reliable air conditioning. Seated with a plate of *arroz con pollo* and Cuban lager to revive us as we watched sun-fried tourists rush back to cruise ships, I thought of my aunt Elena and realized that she probably didn't have many memories of her own of Havana. She was around four or five years old in 1959, and she didn't visit Cuba until 2018, so whatever she told me about Havana before my visit came from family anecdotes, secondhand stories of others who had been, and whatever reports she was used to hearing from the travel industry. It was odd to think that the living, breathing *Frommer's Guide to Everywhere* had such little experience of, yet managed to characterize so well, a very popular neighborhood in her hometown, a few miles away from the hospital where she was born and the church where she was baptized.

Among her siblings, my mother, Carmen, is the one with the best memory of their Cuba, and her stories humanize Cuba in a way that makes it feel familiar. My mother refers to the gleaming white Mendoza House as "my grandmother's house," but her sister has tracked the Mendoza House across all its illustrious press. They have processed their memories in very different ways. For my mother, Cuba is a part of her childhood, and for my aunt, Cuba is an adventure to be explored. Both perspectives intrigue me, but since my ideas about Cuba were formed by the snapshots handed down from Grandma, I was curious about my grandmother's neighborhood of Miramar. Would I be able to find the house that my grandmother grew up in, before she married my grandfather and stepped into her preordained role as a proper Cuban lady?

But when I asked about Miramar, Grandma couldn't remember the address of her house. She couldn't give me landmarks, street names, a nearby park, nothing. Of course, by the time I asked her, she was in her late eighties. Nearly sixty years had passed since her feet had touched Cuban soil. Fidel Castro's regime had changed street names, altered neighborhoods, and erased the Cuba that my grandmother knew, so even if she remembered the street name and could describe the house down to the windowpanes, I still might not have been able to find it. I was initially baffled by her response, but then I realized that there was a lot more attached to this question for my grandmother than an address in Miramar; this was the first time I ever asked her a direct question about life in Cuba before she was married. Previous tales of Cuba centered on my mother and her siblings, not on my grandmother. Maybe her childhood home faded in her memory because she had made a home of her own. Maybe as the mother of five children during a historical revolution, she had to make space in her brain for more critical things. Maybe the house was torn down and the street names changed on purpose so that a proper Cuban lady like my grandmother could never find her way back. Maybe the person she was then needed to fade away to make room for the person she would become.

"I am her memory," my mother said when I asked if it would be worth it to ask Grandma, now in her nineties, about Cuba. When I was a child, my grandmother's stories about Cuba were snapshots from long ago, but when my mother told me her stories from Cuba, the tales were vivid and nuanced, with a charming sweetness that only a seven-year-old's perspective can bring. And that seven-year-old's tales center around a rambling one-story house with tall palm trees towering over the roof. This was the house that my grandparents bought after they were married. They were supposed to have lived in that house forever, to raise their family and to live their lives. This was the first house that my mom, Carmen, and my aunt Elena called home. My grandmother showed me a sepia-toned photo when I was a teenager, and shortly before my trip to Cuba, a digital version of the same photo landed in my inbox from Elena.

"Our home was located in a section called La Colonella," wrote my aunt in an email, and in the upper righthand corner of the photo, I noticed my grandmother's distinctive handwriting noted "June 16, '54." My mother was two and a half years old.

Family legend has it that my grandfather saw the house's address in a *Lonely Planet* guidebook for Cuba where it was noted as the address for a museum. But when my grandmother's older brother attempted to locate their house in La Coronela on a return trip to Cuba, he couldn't find it because of the street names changing. I imagined my great uncle lost in the Havana suburbs as he tried to remember the route to his sister's house when his map no longer matched the street signs. Imagine becoming lost in the place that was once your home. What he remembered soon became meaningless in this new and strange Cuba, and this trip was not that long after the revolution. Not surprisingly, my mom couldn't recall an address for her house when I asked her.

"And it doesn't matter," she said in her matter-of-fact way, "everything has changed."

One night in Havana, Todd and I sat on the Airbnb roof under a full moon, drank more Cuban lager graciously purchased through the black market by our hostess, and flipped through the photos on my phone. When I came across the photo of the house in La Coronela, Todd said, "We've been here for four days and we haven't seen any houses that look like that."

I had to agree. From what we had seen of Havana's architecture in just a day or two, you knew where you were by the architecture around you. The house in La Coronela didn't fit any style we had seen, which made me wonder if we were looking in the wrong place. La Coronela itself proved to be elusive; my own family members had spelled the neighborhood as both "La Colonela" and "La Coronella," already suggesting confusion about what was located where. Unlike my great-grandmother María Mendoza's house, which we stumbled upon on our second day in Havana, my mother's house didn't seem like it was going to magically appear. And unlike the palatial Mendoza House, which didn't look like any place that I could call "home," my mother's house in the photo looked and felt familiar. I heard the rustling wind in the palm trees overhead. I felt the sun beating down on the driveway. Studying the photo under a Cuban full moon, it hit me that the house looked familiar because it looked like *my* grandmother's house—Grandma Faraway's *L*-shaped house in Louisiana. Perhaps fueled by too much beer, I had a strange vision of the house in La Coronela ripping its foundation up, taking flight, soaring over the Gulf of Mexico, and planting itself in the red dirt of central Louisiana. I found the chicken-and-egg scenario amusing: from my perspective the house in Cuba looked like the house in Louisiana, when really it was the other way around.

On our last day in Cuba, we commissioned Alejandro—*"Alex, por favor"*—and his 1952 Dodge with a Hyundai steering wheel and a Toyota engine to drive us to the beach at Santa María del Mar, about forty-five minutes outside of Havana. We nicknamed the car "Frankenstein" and in my halting Spanish with a bit of pantomime and sound effects, we made Alex chuckle at the reference. As the city receded and the flat countryside expanded in front of Frankenstein's dash, I squinted at one-story buildings off in the distance. Was La Coronela around here? Or down that road? How close or how far away am I to my mother's house?

That day at the beach in Santa María del Mar was a memorable, peaceful day in my life. Near the ocean on a beach, I feel humbled by the powerful waves, anchored to the earth, and living in the present. I also felt a strong connection to my mom, because Carmen showed me and my brother how to beach. In my earliest memories, we would arrive at dawn to the briny South Carolina beaches and stay until the sun went down. We dragged umbrellas, chairs, SPF 55, and snacks out to our beach homestead. Once camp was established, my mom became one with her beach chair. Then she turned a dark shade of brown as she sank into a carefree present. The Office of Mom was closed; snacks were in the bag, drinks were in the cooler, don't forget to reapply sunscreen, have a nice day. Watching her on the beach on those marathon days taught me to find perspective, and I didn't realize how much I needed this in Cuba until I was slathering on my third coat of sunscreen under the shade of a two-dollar rented umbrella.

My swirling thoughts settled. Maybe my family's roots in Cuba had flown with the house over the Gulf of Mexico, but I had found a lot more of myself in Cuba than I thought. Settled on my beach chair, I let the past go and focused on taking in as much Cuba as possible before our flight the next day. There was so much to catch my attention. A small restaurant on the beach sent out a guitarist every few hours to serenade us for a dollar and dispatched waiters to bring us beer and water. We watched in amazement as a local fisherman slipped into a wetsuit and dove head-first into the surf. When he emerged, he held up one large, impressive fish and looked so convincing as a warrior of the sea that I looked for his trident. A little later, the waiter handed us a lunch menu, and we learned that the kill was *pargo*. Lightly battered and fried, Triton's *pargo* and a cold beer made an unforgettable lunch.

Reluctant to leave yet knowing that Alex had pulled Frankenstein into the parking lot to ferry us back to Vedado, I pulled a sundress over my bathing suit and looked out towards the ocean. A little boy scurried in front of my camera lens at the water's edge and turned his back to me to watch the horizon. His bathing suit was an American flag. The entire image was just a little too on-the-nose; Santa María del Mar is situated almost directly south of Key West. With my husband telling Alex to wait a moment more, I snapped a photo of a little Cuban boy wrapped in an American flag as he faced the United States.

Not remembering is different from forgetting. My family hasn't forgotten Cuba or their homes and lives there, but they didn't cling to details such as addresses or houses that no longer felt like theirs. They brought over what they could, whether it was a floor plan for a house to build or a tradition of beach visits. Maybe instead of trying to preserve a past that was fading away, it was better to put energy into looking at the present around you, bringing with you what you could, and looking to the horizon. Maybe the Cuba that I saw was unrecognizable to my family, but ultimately what mattered might not have been houses but experiences, memories, and heritage.

El Café es Muy Importante

A coffee cup can hold a complete story of heritage. At least it does for me.

All my life, I've risen around sunrise, made a cup of milky coffee—*café con leche a la Barb*—and sat still in the morning darkness, sometimes with a book, a newspaper, my Kindle, or my journal. My energy comes up as the coffee goes down, the fuse burning to the end, igniting my day. I have watched my mom start her day with a pot of coffee shared with my dad, and I have watched her take her afternoon break with a cup of tea or a latte. My father loves coffee too, but my mom and I hold it sacred, a signal to our system to pause and be with ourselves for a fleeting moment before modern life pounces.

Once my grandmother Barbara remarked to me, "You really love coffee. You can't survive without it. That must be the Cuban side!" She's right: if actions are genetic, then creating a moment of solace with a cup of coffee is Cuban for me. Visiting my Cuban grandparents, I observed their unique coffee rituals too. My grandfather sipped Community Coffee, a brand specific to Louisiana, from a "Valle Farm china cup"—a plastic yellow mug—while he sat in a rocking chair on the camphouse porch. The family orbited around him, the horses' tails swatted flies, the cows chewed, and Abuelito sipped his coffee. Like mine and my mom's coffee rituals, my grandmother, her coffee cup, and her modest bathrobe with its big sash created a moment of serenity before dawn. In the afternoon, my grandmother invited others to share her coffee ritual; while the ice clinked in my glass of homemade cold brew one stormy summer afternoon, Grandma taught me and my brother how to play dominoes. Before I had any connections to Cuba, before I asked my mom about her childhood, and before I knew where Cuba was on a map, I had my morning cup of coffee. So *el café es muy importante* because it is a direct line to my Cuban heritage.

Even our Airbnb in Havana had a coffee ritual. As was his habit because he was married to me, Todd searched the Airbnb upon arrival for coffee supplies. He hoped a Mr. Coffee, a French press, a stovetop espresso machine, a Keurig, or something would appear, but in Havana, Todd came up empty-handed. After a bit of a frantic search, he nervously asked me, "I don't know how we're going to make coffee in the morning." I smiled. Something told me not to worry about coffee in Cuba.

Sure enough, coffee was the next day's opening act. A cheery "*Buenos Dias!*" sounded from downstairs, and our hosts appeared with strong sweet coffee in sturdy mugs, a small pitcher of warm milk, and a glass jar of real sugar cubes. We had nearly finished our first cup when the food arrived along with a second mug of coffee that we wanted but didn't have to ask for. Seated outside on the rooftop deck listening to the sounds of Vedado coming to life and savoring a fresh morning breeze with our coffee made the moment sacred.

In Cuba almost every dish or drink I sampled sent me through a time warp to my grandmother's tiled kitchen where my brother and I were introduced to Cuban dishes such as *pan de medianoche, picadillo,* and *arroz con pollo.* My mom didn't cook Cuban food at home in South Carolina, so when we visited my grandparents, mealtimes felt like a trip to Cuba itself. Grandma made everything with no recipe book and no notes, and she put my curiosity to work adding beer to *arroz con pollo* or laying out the correct flat bowls for *picadillo.* Years later, the *arroz con pollo* at a restaurant behind an art gallery in Vedado arrived in a steamy cloud laced with the scents of garlic, saffron, and beer. The dish smelled so much like Grandma's that the years vanished, carried away on a fragrant chicken-and-rice cloud. A few weeks after we returned home from Cuba, I made *arroz con pollo* myself for the first time, using no recipe and no notes, only my vivid memory of Grandma in her kitchen and my recent amazing experience in Vedado.

Not far from the restaurant behind the art gallery was Café Madrigal, a flamingo pink three-story Victorian house turned into a café, bar, and music venue. Café Madrigal served fruity sangría in a tall, fluted glass on the second-story porch. The cool, refreshing taste was so familiar that I recalled a beach trip to Florida where Grandma directed me and my aunt Barbie as we made an amazing sangría. She didn't use a recipe card for the sangría either, but on the second-story porch, the bubbly, citrusy wine of Café Madrigal made me imagine a recipe card from the early 1950s. I could almost see a rumpled index card dotted with purple wine splotches on which Grandma in her distinct script had jotted down a recipe to mix rioja, brandy, fresh lemonade, and Sprite. Serve over ice. Maybe Grandma had passed the sangría recipe to a friend at a luncheon at the house that became Café Madrigal. Maybe the card had tumbled down and wedged itself in the floorboards of the café, only to be found years later when the soon-to-be café proprietors were doing a walkthrough with the guys who were going to renovate the floors.

Coming off the amazing success with my own attempt at *arroz con pollo*, and with so many dishes resurrected from my archeological palate, I started cooking a lot of Cuban food myself. I did have to turn to the internet for certain things, but my powerful sense memories from childhood and from the trip to Cuba could be relied upon for authentication. *Pan de medianoche*, the sweet eggy bread for Cuban sandwiches, was a challenge that I took up after revisiting and remastering most of the classics. My grandmother never made *pan de medianoche* herself, and when it appeared on the table in Louisiana, this version was never quite right. It's funny to me that what I remember of the *pan de medianoche* in Louisiana wasn't the taste at all; it was the half-moon shape and the yellowy color. The *pan de medianoche* that I ate in Cuba came in all shapes, sizes, and colors but was so delicious that I knew I could never forget it. Using real *pan de medianoche* as my reference point, I set out to establish the world's inaugural *Pan de Medianoche* Competition. I was the sole competitor.

Maybe one reason that my grandmother never attempted to make it herself has to do with the fact that bread is hard to make and master. Among my prized possessions is a Cuisinart bread machine, my not-so-secret weapon in the imaginary bread-making competition. But figuring out the right combination of eggs, sugar, lard, and flour, and the timing of when to add each ingredient so that the dough came out sweet but not cakey and sturdy enough to support roast pork, sliced ham, sliced pickles, and cheese felt like advanced engineering, voodoo, rocket science, and dumb luck. For several consecutive Sundays one dark, dreary New York winter, while others were Netflixing and pretending New Year's diet resolutions still mattered, I trudged the snowy Queens sidewalks in search of blocks of lard, two dozen eggs, and a twelve-pound bag of sugar. Lights blazed in my kitchen/bakery while lard and sugar heated on the stove and I beat eggs to death. The bread machine danced on the counter to its own rhythmic cycles of "mix," "rise," "rest," "mix number two," "rise number two," *cha, cha, cha*. The small loaves that popped out of my four-hundred-degree oven a few hours later were carbohydrate gold.

The next day, I bundled myself and trudged through the mucky New York City wintry mix to deliver two fresh mini loaves to Sara the Real Cuban, who was the only judge in the *Pan de Medianoche* Competition. Thanks to her candid feedback and encouragement, I tweaked the recipe until I was declared the hands-down winner of the world's first *Pan de Medianoche* Competition. The hard part over, I could focus my efforts on the other elements of the Cuban sandwich. The roast pork was easy; I leaned on my Southern roots for the basics, and the rest was just interpretation. Just as I found the right brand of lard for the bread at a South American grocery a few blocks away from my apartment, Todd and I learned through trial and error that kosher half-sour pickles, brown New York City deli mustard, and manchego cheese would round it out. Between mouthfuls, Sara the Real Cuban said, "This is an amazing Cuban sandwich, Barb, because it's *your* Cuban sandwich." Not only had I made a good one but figuring it out for myself apparently cemented my win in the mind of the only judge.

As the pink blooms were busting out on the two trees in front of my apartment, I celebrated my victory in my imaginary competition with a few long Saturday afternoon hikes and some extra hours with the barbell after weeks of sampling lard and roasting pork. I had won a key battle with myself and what it meant to me to be Cuban. Mastering Cuban cooking was a big deal for me, and I had great fun making something that was authentically Cuban, authentically me, and freaking delicious.

Calling myself Cuban American has been difficult for me because I carried an unspoken and vague list of what it meant to be Cuban, a set of arbitrary and invented qualifications that

I thought I didn't meet. When I moved to New York and met Cuban Americans not from my extended family, the Real Cubans gave me permission to dismiss these assumptions. Visiting Cuba was a chance to banish these ideas once and for all. In Cuba, I never felt as if I didn't belong, and after the trip, I felt empowered to try on the label *Cuban American* for myself. My adventures in cooking were the way I proved to myself that I could embrace my heritage and share it with the world. Sandwiches, coffee, and all the comfort foods that I had grown up with were important first steps, but it was just the door opening. Things that I didn't expect to have any connection to Cuba at all but made up the foundation of me were revealed as very Cuban.

When I was six, I asked my mom to enroll me in ballet lessons, and for the next twelve years, my life centered on ballet classes, rehearsals, and annual recitals. Long after I had retired my pointe shoes and shortly after the trip to Cuba, I attended an outdoor yoga class in Central Park with a group of colleagues. After class, a young woman I barely knew approached me, introduced herself, and asked me if I was a dancer. She was asking because she had noticed my arm movements and hip flexibility during yoga class. I told her my name and said yes, I had a lot of ballet experience from childhood and the movement patterns were ingrained.

Her face lit up and she smiled. Then she asked, "Your name is Barbara and you studied ballet? Are you from Miami?"

(By the way, if you ask my mom if she's from Miami, she bristles. "Why does everyone assume I'm from Miami?" she asks with an annoyed huff. I once promised her a T-shirt with this phrase that she could wear on the beach in Miami.)

But I knew exactly what this new friend was getting at that evening in Central Park. "No, I'm not from Miami but my mom is from Cuba."

"Well, that makes total sense," she said. Her father was from Cuba, and she had grown up in Miami, where every Cuban

American girl she knew took ballet and piano lessons, occasionally under duress. Sara the Real Cuban had visited me again.

I laughed and told her a story about Grandma on a visit to South Carolina. I was a few months into my study of ballet, and Grandma, showing real enthusiastic interest, not just humoring a child, asked for a demonstration. As I contorted through the five basic positions, she joined me. Suddenly there was an impromptu *barre* on the patio to the *clickety-clack* of my brother's scooter wheels and the *slurpy-slurp* from the family dog at her water bowl. My agile grandmother moved as if she herself had finished ballet class a few hours ago. Then, she told me stories about her ballet lessons at what would become Alicia Alonso's world-famous Cuban National Ballet School. I imagined that her ballet school looked a little bit like mine: shiny hardwood floors, blue cinder block walls, and thick wooden barres bolted to the wall with iron brackets. Through the windows near the ceiling at my studio, I saw the tops of pine trees, but she probably saw coconut-laden tall palms. Color drained from my mental image to better resemble the sepia-toned photos from Cuba in photo albums, and a cluster of tiny Cuban ballerinas who really didn't look all that different from my cluster of tiny Southern ballerinas appeared. At my ballet class the following week, I introduced myself as "Carmelina the Ballerina," owning my first name for the first time.

When I asked for ballet lessons, I had no idea about ballet and its prominent place in Cuban culture and I didn't know my grandmother had studied ballet herself, but years later, when Sara the Real Cuban, disguised as a total stranger, noticed how I moved my arms in a yoga class and approached me with a few questions, I learned something about myself as a Cuban American. Long before I went to Cuba, I had started to challenge those old qualifications of what it meant to be Cuban and replace it all with a new list. Resilience, focus, good humor, reliability, creativity, authenticity, discipline, and intensity are values that I see in Cubans that go beyond skin tone and language skills. These magical moments where a bit of Cuba has been excavated help me to shed my made-up qualifications and made me think I was part of the Cuban American patchwork.

As a child, I was told that my family was not Hispanic. I was told that although we had ancestors in Cuba for hundreds of years, the family traces its roots to Spain, so we are Spanish. *Yeah, just like Memah is Irish,* I smirked to myself. In 2021, I gathered my courage to attend a panel hosted by and featuring Latinx and Hispanic professionals during Hispanic Heritage Month. I took a leap to put myself in the presence of people who self-identified in a way that I hadn't. I signed up thinking that I would finally get some answers from the panelists. They knew exactly who they were and where they came from, and by hearing what they had to share, I would finally have some answers about me.

It started off on solid footing. Right at the top of the hour, the panel addressed the terms "Latinx" and "Hispanic" and the difference between the two. Within five minutes, while the audience was still settling in, a question that I had carried for years was answered. The moderator said, "If your family came from Spain or Portugal to the Americas, then you are Hispanic." She then went on to say that Latinx, Latino, and Latina refer to people with ancestors from the Americas. I would have shrieked for joy but the panel continued: no matter how long ago my ancestors from Spain arrived in Cuba, I still carry that distinction. Coming to the United States via Cuba also makes the word *Hispanic* more applicable than *Spanish,* yet it also doesn't transform my family from *Hispanic* to *Latinx.* I redeemed something that night when I heard that. But then I quickly learned that I was lucky to have a label that fit. I was not alone in coming to the panel with a load of confusion and baggage; the moderator, the panelists, and a vocal portion of the audience did too. When it became clear to me that I was not getting a multiple-choice quiz to assess my score on the Cuban heritage scale, I put down my pencil and I just listened. And what I heard sounded very familiar:

When I visit family in South America, I'm very aware of my light skin.

People have told me that I look Trinidadian, but I'm not. I'm Puerto Rican.

I am Haitian American. I don't even speak Spanish. Why am I considered Latino?

What I had begun to articulate for myself in private, quiet places was being presented to me by those who had—in my view—figured it all out. And rather than feeling frustration and anger over not finding answers, I felt a huge sense of relief. We're all dealing with the same issues and the same questions, and it feels as if we all have the same story. How we live our lives is how we live our culture. It is ingrained in the smallest things that we do, and it can't fully dissolve into the melting pot. Because she was raising me, my mom showed me how to live, and how she lived was very Cuban at the heart of it, despite pressure to melt into the United States.

Having spent a portion of her life in the South, my mother faced examples of what she was supposed to be, and what she was supposed to be was not Cuban. Being Hispanic was not something you embraced; it was going to hold you back. She was not supposed to speak Spanish anymore, and her children definitely weren't. She never met anyone in the South who was interested in her story or interested in who she was. When my parents moved away from South Carolina, my mother met her own Sara the Real Cuban and other people who were interested in her story, who didn't assume she was from Miami, and who were curious to get to know her as a Cuban-born American.

My mother's story is one of assimilation, whereas mine is one of differentiation. How hard did she have to work to blend in, yet how hard do I have to work to stand out? It couldn't have been any easier for her than for me, but as I watched my mom live her life, I learned to live mine and learned to survive other people's ignorance. I have watched minds blow up when I say that I am Cuban American. When I was still spouting the excuses of sunburn and not speaking Spanish, I watched as the blue eyes of the man who would become my husband grew wide in amazement. I shared this on our first date, even though I was still defining who I was for myself, knowing that his reaction would tell me a lot about him. I could see that I had caught him off guard, but I also saw that challenging his assumptions was not threatening to him. He was curious and interested in the honest, open-hearted way that he was curious and interested in so many things, and he wanted to learn and know more about me, about my connection to Cuba, and about Cuba itself.

Over the years he has been the biggest supportive witness to my journey. Todd takes it all to the next level: at home, he bought me a coffee pot with a timer. He prepares the coffee the night before and sets the timer for me so it pops on before I am awake. He bought me a coffee mug with the name "Carmelina" on it for my birthday. He has followed me to every restaurant, listened to every rant, eaten everything I put in front of him, nearly died from lard overdoses, met every relative, asked the stupid questions, and encouraged every bit of storytelling and reminiscing. He embraced my love of travel, and after meeting my aunt Elena a few months before our wedding, he made a comment that traveling and taking journeys was genetic. I might never have made the connection that traveling to find out more about this world meant finding out more about myself if Todd had not connected those dots between me and my aunt.

In January 2017 as the JetBlue ticketing confirmation popped up in my email, I told him—yes, *told*—that we were going to Havana for five days, he responded, "Vamoose!" After a split second's confusion, I laughed.

"You mean *vámanos*," I explained.

"*Vámanos*," he repeated. "What does that mean?"

"Let's go."

En la Casa de la Abuela de mi Madre

In the canon of family lore that I share with my parents and brother, my father, Tony, has a famous story. My mother was keeping their engagement a secret from her parents. As my father told it, she took her ring off when she visited her family. This went on long enough for my grandmother Barbara to ask my dad, "Well, are you getting married or not?"

Born in South Carolina a few months after my mother was born in Havana, my father was the third of six children. The Cavers are a staunchly Catholic, scrappy bunch. My dad has said that he should have been a hippie since he was a teenager in the 1960s, but he also missed Woodstock by three years. One of his favorite songs is Iron Butterfly's "In-a-Gadda-Da-Vida" from 1967, when he was the quarterback for the high school football team coached by the man I called Grandaddy. My father followed his college football dream until he decided that his brain was a better investment than his brawn, and after earning his college degree, he became a veterinarian. In the throes of vet school's punishing workload, he decided to blow off steam and drove eight hours in a car he called the Flintstone Car to visit his cousin in New Orleans to party for the weekend. There he was set up on a blind date with his cousin's college roommate. Carmen del Valle, my mother.

I don't know much about who my mother was as a young woman the night she met my father. I don't know her favorite song from high school, and her college experience in New Orleans in the early 1970s was surprisingly uneventful. As a parent, she was self-possessed, independent, and content to do what she called "her own thing." But until Carmen chose to marry Tony, she had never really done her own thing. So much was chosen for her, and she had to deal with it. My father has always celebrated my mother for doing her own thing, so I think committing to life with my dad was a no-brainer. Still, I imagine that the engagement ring coming on and off might have been Carmen's way of getting used to the idea of a choice that would be hers and hers alone, like dipping your feet in the ocean to test the temperature of the water and pull of the undertow. Lucky for me, she jumped in and swam.

Though the details are fluid, the bones of Tony's famous story are the same. My parents agreed on a time to tell Grandma and Abuelito about their engagement. My mom went to the master suite at the opposite end of the *L*-shaped house to tell them, while my father remained in the living room with my uncle.

Suddenly, my father heard a squabble like fighting between cats and dogs break out. My father said to my uncle that it was time to go back there, and my uncle replied, "Good luck."

When Tony jumped into the fray, the first question Abuelito asked was, "What is your inheritance?"

To which my father responded, "You're looking at it."

I've heard the story many times, sometimes retelling it myself and sometimes as the little kid eavesdropping at the door. Tony tells it like a great actor commanding his audience with grand gestures and sound effects, and Carmen shakes her head in bemusement. In one version of the story, my dad inverted his pockets and out fell the keys to the Flintstone Car and three balls of lint. (Carmen might take that opportunity to make a comment from the peanut gallery such as, "There were also two dimes.") Often my dad would quip that being Catholic was the only thing he had going for him. (Carmen would nod.) Once, after watching *The Princess Bride*, he compared himself to the stable boy trying to win the hand of the princess. Fresh off the tennis court, my mother unlaced her sneakers and tossed dirty socks and sweatbands into the washing machine. That time she said something like, "*princess,* yeah, right."

I was a young adult when my father told me how my grandfather's question about inheritance made him feel.

"What did he mean, inheritance?" my father said when he and I were drinking beer at an alehouse in Brooklyn. He was in New York for a conference and I was at the start of my career. Twenty-seven years had passed since Abuelito asked my father that question, and it seemed like my father was still trying to answer it. Why was the idea of inheritance so important to Abuelito? The question was odd and . . . insulting. We weren't living in medieval Spain, and if I were my dad, I wonder what I would have done. Maybe I would have tried to take the high road, summoning more equanimity and patience than a hostage negotiator to attempt to explain with the goal of reaching a mutual understanding, or maybe I would have responded the same way he did, scooping up the dimes with a "bless your heart" thrown in for good measure.

Inheritance to me meant something earned, not something given. Inheritance, as I think Abuelito meant it, carried with it some degree of control and expectation that made me squirm. During the conversation in the master suite with the three balls of lint bouncing on the floor, my parents were college-educated young adults pursuing professional careers; while a check or gift from their parents as a blessing on their union would have been appreciated, my parents clearly expected to build their life together without any expectations for what it had to look like or who they had to be. For them, marriage was jumping into the ocean and swimming along together. And they wanted to do it not because there was anything to gain but because they loved each other.

Abuelito's question said a lot about what he valued, so exploring it was a way to understand what made him tick. The question of inheritance and why it was so important had to tie in to Cuba; Abuelito's first future son-in-law was very American and thought of inheritance in a totally different way. This perspective was passed down to me, Abuelito's first and very American granddaughter and his wife's namesake. Barely twenty years after my grandparents left Cuba, so much had changed in the cultural landscape of the world.

In 2017, I stood at the corner of Calle 15 and Paseo in Havana, looking at something that my ancestors built. By then, I had established a life of my own with support from my family but largely accomplished through my own actions and choices. For me, inheritance looked like emotional support and respect, not like the beautiful white mansion in front of me. The man who commissioned and owned this impressive residence was my great-great-grandfather, "wealthy banker Pablo González de Mendoza" according to the *Havana Times*. Wealthy banker Pablo's daughter was María Mendoza, and María's son was Abuelito.

This house might have been HIS.

If Castro's revolution hadn't forced my family into exile in the United States, Abuelito might have inherited this house with its indoor glassed-in swimming pool and lush manicured courtyard. In the shadow of the giant ornate *M* atop the gates, I saw the question that Abuelito posed to my father in a different way.

Though it wasn't this house in Abuelito's dreams, it became clear to me that he grew up knowing that he was entitled to something opulent, something that would take a lifetime for others to build, something that was out of reach for so many more. What he stood to inherit was a tangible example of great privilege. Inheritance might not have looked like this for my father or for me, but it was a big, white, mansion-sized deal to my Abuelito Carlos del Valle, grandson of Pablo González de Mendoza.

Abuelito loomed large as patriarch, and while he commanded respect, I often wondered what he had done to earn it. When I think of what I knew of Abuelito's work, career, and family life in the United States and how everything he accomplished should have been such a great source of pride for him, I wondered why an old-fashioned notion like inheriting a big fancy house with a platoon of forks was so important. Abuelito escaped political upheaval, brought his family to a new country, and educated his children. He was a homeowner and business owner. If it sounds like the American Dream, then maybe that's because it is, and it has a lot in common with the lives that my Southern grandparents lived. When Castro's goons held him up at gunpoint and told him to leave Cuba and never return, he didn't hang around to get shot. He about-faced and flew back to his wife and five kids in Lake Placid, which I think speaks volumes about his priorities, yet he still clung to a culture that had violently ended. Ultimately, I wonder if Abuelito ever said to himself, "You know what? The world changed, but I am still here. I am thriving here, and so is my family." The fact that maybe he couldn't do that for himself is a great tragedy. If he had been able to change his narrative like that, what kind of man would I have known?

As it stands today, the Mendoza House is unique among the mishmash of derelict ruins, works-in-progress modern construction, and painstakingly restored Spanish colonial and Victorian architecture throughout Havana. The vintage cars speeding by on the Malecón made my dad's first car look like a Ferrari. On a side street in the middle of central Havana, we stepped aside to let two rickety carts pulled by mules pass by. Although they looked like they had dropped into Havana from late 1800s Spain, the mules *clop-clopped* along unfazed by the traffic and packed city buses. One mule cart delivered cases of black-market Blue Moon beer to a bar flying the flag of an Australian rugby club.

I heard that Havana was frozen in time, but on the day I understood what the Mendoza House meant for my family, I realized I couldn't quite pinpoint the time in which we were frozen. Sure, the cars looked like they drove out of the 1950s, but the mule carts called to mind the 1870s, and the buildings looked like everything from 1920s Art Deco Miami Beach to 1980s Cold War Budapest. A better description was anachronistic. Havana was a mishmash of eras that together make a large mosaic of Cuban history. In a short period of time, the changes that came to Havana were volatile, and my family rode the waves as best as they could. They moved on as best as they could. What is frozen in time in Havana is the Mendoza House, standing in all its glory as a monument to a time long ago.

That night in Vedado was surprisingly cool and breezy, so we settled at Café Madrigal for what I called Carmelina Sangría and live music from a band called La Floridita. Café Madrigal dates from the 1920s when the original house was probably, like the Mendoza House, commissioned by a wealthy Havana businessman as a visual symbol of the family's status. There the similarities end. During Castro's regime, the Mendoza House became the residence of the British ambassador to Cuba, and Café Madrigal was converted into an apartment building. In the late 1990s, an inch of private enterprise was allowed, and the structure was restored as best as possible to its original 1920s appearance. It began a new life as a café, bar, and music venue.

Stories like this abound through Cuba, especially in Vedado and other parts of Havana.

The band took a break and we could hear music from the café across the street named *El Submarino Amarillo* (the Yellow Submarine). Our waitress brought another round, caught us singing along, and smiled. "Cubans love the Beatles," she said in halting English, then again in Spanish. The Beatles were one of many bands, television shows, and films from other countries banned by the Castro regime as a means of controlling information and only recently allowed into Cuba. Our waitress explained that Fidel's niece Mariela Castro famously quotes John Lennon and is a big fan. I clocked how the Beatles went from banned to celebrated in less than sixty years. In the twenty-five years between Abuelito's marriage to my grandmother and my parents' wedding, the word *inheritance* changed its appearance several times. History seemed to be rushing cultural change from generation to generation at a fast pace, and I needed to catch my breath.

I took my sangría to the porch on the highest floor while my husband purchased La Floridita's CD. Surrounding the quaint square are houses in every stage of restoration and collapse imaginable; during the day, the drone of construction filled the air, but now at night, I noticed a different scene. Some of the houses were blazing light and humming with music while others were totally dark, waiting for old life to return to them or for new life to transform them. I wondered, who else valued, dreamed of, and pined for these houses? Who else's inheritance was visible from where I was standing? Certainly not mine.

The idea of the Mendoza House as my inheritance was so absurd that I laughed out loud. I tried to picture myself living in the Mendoza House, and I couldn't. I tried to picture my mom living in the Mendoza House, and I couldn't. I tried to picture myself as a teenager visiting my grandparents at the Mendoza House, and I couldn't. Not even my vivid imagination could put us there, except as tourists peering through the wrought iron gates. I could only picture the Mendoza House as the home of my ancestors from another era so removed from my experience that it might as well have been historical fiction. Why had they put their dreams into a house? A house that was taken away from them by people who thought the Beatles were dissident. This was the first time that I thought about the impact of Fidel Castro's revolution in a way that wasn't just academic and removed from me: if Fidel Castro's revolution had not happened, my grandfather might have inherited something like the Mendoza House. But if Fidel Castro's revolution had not happened, then I never would have been born.

Maybe my brain was soaked in sangría, but I found myself imagining another version of myself. Barbara, María Mendoza del Valle's great-granddaughter, born in Havana in September 1979 . . . and I didn't get very far with this image. There was no alternative to the way my life had unfolded. How was the Mendoza House and all that it stood for supposed to have survived? That night on the balcony of Café Madrigal, I realized that I had been denied my inheritance. Not a big fancy house, nor access to elite parties on the Malecón, nor any antiquated, Downton-Abbey-in-the-tropics dowry. Because my family's status forced them into exile, because governments slam doors on not just people but generations, I had been missing a huge Cuba-sized jewel piece in my inheritance. Yet here I was. Sipping sangría just a few blocks away from my great-grandmother's house. Here not because I was obligated to be, but because I wanted to be. Here through my own courage and means. That night, the score was "Barbara - 1, Fidel - 0" as Beatles music floated through the air.

Barbara María Mendoza would have had a very good life if Castro's revolution had never happened. She planned great parties for her father's and husband's businesses in the Mendoza House. Her best friend lived at the house currently occupied by

Café Madrigal, which never existed. Barbara and her BFF drank *café con leche* at a café in the shadow of the Ballet Nacional de Cuba where their daughters were in ballet class together. She attended school in the United States, had a home in Spain, and was fluent in English. The same money that built the Mendoza House would have given Barbara María Mendoza all of the things that Carmelina Barbara Caver worked for and attained: education, career, travel, independence. All of which brought me back to Cuba, like a salmon trying to swim upstream. Here I was on a warm March night, running around Vedado, eating *arroz con pollo*, listening to music. And I felt as if parallel timelines were converging. Just like the ghostly face in my photo of the Mendoza House, I started to see faint traces of my family's footprints. Footprints that I feel I have walked in quite well, even though their version of inheritance and mine look a bit different.

On the flight back to New York from Cuba, I tried again to picture myself as a descendant of Pablo González de Mendoza, but not in a world where the revolution never happened, in the world of today. And a question popped into my head: *What if I ever get the keys to my great-grandmother's house?* Suddenly I could see the giant wrought iron gates with the fancy *M* on top opening for me. If there exists a future where the Mendoza House is returned to me or to my cousins, no matter how distant, I know exactly what I would do. My great-grandmother's house would become an inn for children, grandchildren, and great-grandchildren of the Cuban diaspora who want to learn Spanish and cook Cuban food. I would pack my Cuisinart bread machine and an adapter for Cuban electrical sockets because *pan de medianoche* is first on the recipe list.

If one day you decide to visit Cuba, you find yourself on Trip Advisor or some other website, and you stumble across Casa de María Mendoza, well, I hope you know what you're in for. If you're looking for mojitos on white sand beaches and rides at sunset in Frankencars, you should move on. Casa María offers an unparalleled immersion and exploration into Cuban culture for people who always questioned what it meant to be Cuban. Once you've rinsed off your flight and your first few minutes of Caribbean heat with a float in the pool, you can make your own mojito in the tiled kitchen and take it to the garden. Maybe a mojito or two will tease out your Spanish, maybe not, but whatever your connection to Cuba, *bienvenidos*. If you're here to ask questions and if you're ready for a few answers, then Casa de María might just change your life.

Señora Cuba

A few weeks after my trip to Havana, I dreamed that Cuba was a woman and she spoke to me.

"Hello, Bárbara," she said. Three syllables. "*Mucho gusto.* So nice to meet you."

Her Spanish skipped on the ocean breeze with a musical lilt, the English following like a tugboat. And I found myself unable to answer. The words were lodged deep in my throat.

Señora Cuba was a towering, voluptuous woman with glowing skin and hair like a thundercloud. She wore a red sleeveless dress. On her left hand, she wore one silver ring with a large aquamarine stone. Her eyes were bright. Her size was impossible to comprehend; she was everywhere, immense, and encompassing. I was standing on the Malecón, the concrete spine separating the bustling city of Havana and the crashing waves of the ocean. But Señora Cuba reclined on a low-slung, hammock-like beach chair woven from plantain leaves and white ropes. Thick beach sand blanketed the area around her hammock, deep enough to hide her enormous feet. Her grain-covered toes fanned out from under the sand, and I saw there were eleven toes. A shiny silver ring glinted on the second toe of her left foot.

I vaguely recalled an article in a *National Geographic* magazine from a subscription series that Abuelito had given me; the article described how certain cultures revered people with extra toes as divine figures. Was I in the presence of a divine figure? I started to ask but then I was distracted by a neon pink Chevrolet whizzing so close to me that my hair jumped off my neck. It made a sound like a cartoon elephant trumpeting, not like a car engine from the 1950s. Was I going to be the victim of a Malecón hit-and-run in my own dream?

This was all so strange; here I was, speaking to an eleven-toed goddess on a beach that isn't really a beach while narrowly avoiding dismemberment by bright pink cars that don't sound like cars. What kind of dream was this? The sun was blazing overhead. I ran my hands over my arms; *was I wearing enough sunscreen for this dream? What happened to my hat?* Another car flashed past me, the chrome fins glinting like the fish found in tidal pools. These tiny fish were delicious when deep-fried and served with cold beer. The word came to me: *boquerones*. I tasted the salty crunch and tried to remember the English word. Señora Cuba found my scrambling and clinging for words as entertaining as a crab scuttling over rocks. She chuckled like a roll of thunder and I felt her laugh deep in my belly.

Señora Cuba asked, "*Dígame*, what are we going to talk about?"

What do you say to a goddess who is a place? I found it so hard to speak, to use my voice, to bring what was deep in the shadows into the hot light of the Caribbean sun. One by one, the eleven toes folded down, and the toe ring flashed bright then vanished under the white sand.

On the Malecón you are never alone. People watched the waves crash on the seawall, dodged the breakneck traffic whizzing by, strolled casually, talked loudly, and sipped dark Havana Club from cracked glasses. Even the sun seemed to dance in and out from behind heavy clouds. So much activity, and no one else seemed to notice the short white woman and large goddess on a makeshift beach.

Then, it all faded—the rum, the glasses, the people, the traffic, all of it except the white sun, the salty mist, the crashing surf, and her bright eyes. As if it were being sucked backwards through a vacuum, the Malecón rolled itself up and left me facing Señora Cuba, all alone. I wanted to break the silence. And so in a very important moment, what I said was, "Um, you kinda look like a mural of the Hawaiian goddess Pele that I once saw on the Big Island."

I immediately felt like the world's biggest idiot.

Her face rolled from confusion to amusement to acceptance, then she shrugged and her smile widened. "*Qué linda.* I like it."

But once I started talking, I couldn't stop. Thirty-seven years of questions came tumbling out, "Why don't you look like me? Why don't you sound like me? Why are you so close yet far away? Why are you speaking to me now? Where have you been all my life?" My questions landed hard in the soundless vacuum and Señora Cuba grew solemn.

Then she transformed, compacting and morphing into shapes of people I did and didn't recognize, including myself, until all forms dissipated one by one into the salty mist. When she spoke again, her voice echoed all around me with two overlapping voices: one voice was hers in Spanish, and the other was mine in English.

"There is a space that you inhabit here, in my heart," she said. "Through the centuries I have welcomed so many people, so many ideas, so many ethnicities, so many ideologies. There is room, there is a home, there is safety and security and identity for everyone, but the trials of man tear it all to pieces. *Barbara*,"—three syllables—"I tell you, I reach for every child of mine who thinks that I have forgotten them or that I don't care about them. But I never forget. And I never forgot you. When

I reached for you, you reached back." I felt rather than saw her broad, all-encompassing smile as she said, "And we have a lot to discover about each other, don't we?"

Then I woke up.

As my eyes focused on the light streaming through my apartment, the dream spiraled and swirled away. This was the kind of dream that, despite the high theatrics and absurdity, stuck with me. This was the kind of dream that changes lives. I reached for subtle details long after it had faded. My questions answered by an eleven-toed goddess on a beach that's not real, I realized I had a new adventure in front of me: to journey again and again to the Cuba that resides deep in me.

To change my story was the first step; for so long, I had referred to Cuba as something separate from me. I had learned a lot from my family; for my mother and her siblings, Cuba was a memory. For my grandparents, Cuba was in the tiles on the kitchen floor and hanging on the walls of their home, but the walls and the floor are taken for granted and not often noticed. My grandmother's story, my mother's story, my family's story belongs to them. I have my own version of the Cuban American story to tell, and in that story, I embark on a brave adventure to a forbidden place, curious to know more, and discover that Señora Cuba wanted to know me too. I've traveled to many far-flung places and Cuba is the only one that I remember with all five senses. I can brew a cup of coffee in my apartment in Queens, take a sip, and feel the heat of the sun in Havana.

Before Castro was a blip on the radar, Cuba was inhabited by people who sunburned and people who didn't. Some people refer to themselves as "exiles" and others who didn't leave refer to the same group as "enemies of the state." People read a name on a driver's license and make assumptions. People glance up and see a woman with curly black hair and dark skin carrying a fair-skinned baby girl with curly red hair and make assumptions.

Assumptions are dangerous. I can be very Cuban and not Cuban at all. I can be a Southerner and not very Southern at all. I can be a New Yorker and not very New York at all. It's a bunch of colors smeared together, not a single swatch. It's a tidal pool in constant motion swirling the sands of the beach, not a placid lake. As people we are layered, diverse, and nuanced, and I hope we can always be both curious and careful about our individual complexity.

This is my heritage quest: What started with my legal name continues when I know the *pan de medianoche* needs another egg just by looking at the color of the dough. What started with a cool visa stamp in my passport as my husband and I boarded a plane bound for Havana continues as powerful sensory memories. As I start to forge my own relationship with Cuba, I worry over the political tensions and embargo; it's a three-hour flight from New York and it might as well be completely across the world. I worry that my blond-haired, blue-eyed nephews will never know a word of Spanish except from a textbook and will never hear the story about the goat and its cart on Flor del Valle. Connecting to Cuba, I discover something that is bigger, older, and more permanent than I am.

I don't want to die without ever finding out what it means to be Cuban American. And I hope, with great ego and fire that I think would make Changó/Santa Bárbara proud, that I can be brave enough, big enough, and strong enough to transcend upheaval and render words like *war, revolution, exile,* and *diaspora* meaningless. It seems both insurmountable and simple. This was the message Señora Cuba brought to me in my dreams. She was the agent who stamped my passport as I embarked on this heritage quest, and she showed me that I was standing on a road. In the rearview mirror are the excuses, the qualifiers, the belief that I am not Cuban enough. In front of me is the choice to explore, to learn, and to proudly claim and tell my story.

Acknowledgments

I am happy to acknowledge the following people and places who provided guidance, support, encouragement, and love in my journey to write my first full-length book, starting with the book's formidable and motivational developmental editor (aka book doula) Janna Marlies Maron, Margaret Whitford, Lyra Halprin, Lasell Jaretzki Bartlett, Molly Mogren Katt, Brinn Langdale, Chick Morgan, Marilyn Kiku Guggenheim, Joseph Perry, Ellen Lee, Chris Bertolotti, Nicole Little, Sisa Bueno, Ana Camacho Lord, Susan Henry, Jennifer Davis-Lewis, Mike Ramirez, Eric Salvador, Gregory Gardner, Jackie Carr, Kate Lewin Hilgenberg, Alyssa Reid, Mindy MacInnes, Ashleigh Renard, Joey Garcia, Vicki Mayk and Dawn Leas with the Words in the Sand Writing Retreat, Kelley Monahan Prust, Brooke Warner, Lauren Wise, Julie Metz, Ann Jackson, Corinne Moulder and the team at Smith Publicity, the staff and Open Mic Night patrons of the Queensboro Restaurant in Jackson Heights, my parents Carmen and Tony Caver, John Caver, Sally Caver, Jack Caver, Sam Caver, Elena Countiss, Isabel Carriere, Barbara del Valle Carr, Kelley and Luis del Valle. Saving the best for last, I send a special thank you to my husband Todd Lockwood who tolerated literary widowhood, never complained about the 5 a.m. wake-up calls, and attempts Spanish with an enviable amount of chutzpah.

About the Author

Photo credit: Alissa Randall

Barbara Caver is a lifelong student of the arts and is an accomplished film and television production executive. She loves traveling, exercising, hiking, dancing, cooking, and eating, as well as writing about all of these things with great enthusiasm, affection, and humor. *A Little Piece of Cuba: A Journey to Become Cubana Americana* is her first full-length memoir. Raised in South Carolina, Barbara currently resides in Jackson Heights, New York City.

Looking for your next great read?

We can help!

Visit www.shewritespress.com/next-read
or scan the QR code below for a list
of our recommended titles.

She Writes Press is an award-winning
independent publishing company founded to
serve women writers everywhere.